Translation as a Profession

by

Roger Chriss

ISBN: 978-1-4303-0133-2

Table of Contents

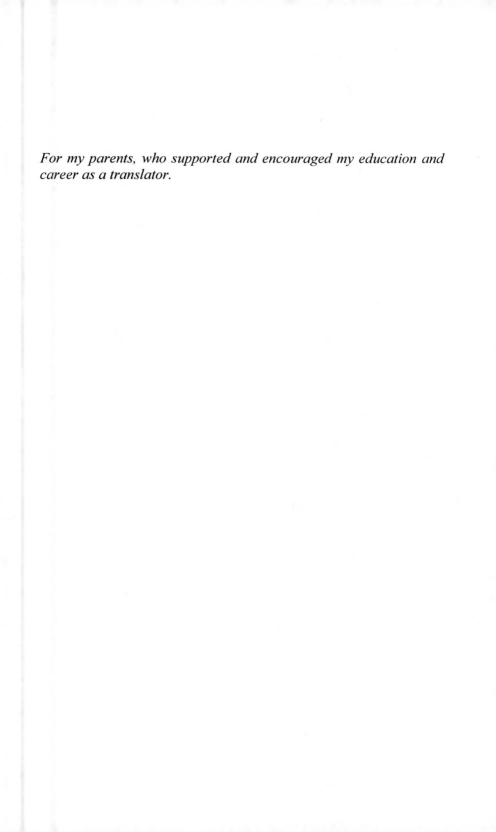

For my parents, who supported and encouraged my education and career as a translator.

Preface

The translation profession has seen rapid growth and change in the past decade in the U.S., going through the dot.com boom when jobs in localization abounded, through bursting of the bubble, when many translators had to rapidly adapt to a new market, loss of jobs, and changes in technology that redefined how they did their work.

With the start of the War on Terror, translators, for perhaps the first time in history, are being interviewed on television and featured in newspaper and magazine articles, there is active recruitment by the U.S. government, in particular the military and intelligence community, and there is increased public awareness of the role translators and translation play in not only national security but modern life in general.

It is, in other words, an exciting time to be a translator, and a good time to join the profession. But despite increased public awareness and interest, plus the active recruiting in the public sector and increased demand in the private sector, little is known about the profession, in particular how to find and keep a good job, whether working for one employer or starting one's own freelance business.

I've been in the translation industry full-time since 1993, though I did my first translation in 1987. After graduating with a M.A. in Japanese translation and interpretation from the Monterey Institute of International Studies in 1993, I went to work as a freelance translator, and had to figure out for myself everything from marketing and business practices, to paying taxes and setting up a retirement plan.

As I learned, I wrote, creating a series of articles called "Translation as a Profession" in 1994 and 1995 for the CompuServe Foreign Language Forum. They were well received, and formed the foundation of a course I taught to translation students on the subject of being a professional translator at the Monterey Institute from 1996 through 2002. In 2000, I rewrote the entire series to bring it up to date with emerging technologies, the changing business landscape, and comments and suggestions from readers and students.

In 2005, I wrote the third edition of the article series, which had at that point been translated into over eight languages and used as course material in several translation schools around the world. I updated the content again to cover the influence of the War on Terror on translators and the effects of maturing technologies, particularly Machine-Assisted Translation tools. The articles were placed in their own home on my web site, The Language Realm (www.languagerealm.com), where they have been read by thousands of people since.

But still this was not enough. The books I've seen on the translation profession are typically too abstract or short to fully prepare a newcomer for the profession, and lack the detailed information everyone experienced in the profession has had to learn one way or another. Further, many of them are written by people without the breadth or depth of experience necessary to fully grasp how the industry works, and therefore how to optimize your chances for success in it.

So I decided to turn the article series into a book that would capture both the industry in its entirety and introduce everything a newcomer would need to know to succeed. I kept the title the same, though the book is far more comprehensive than the article series was, and of course is current as of October, 2006.

The content of this book is based not only on my 14 years of experience in the profession and my education as a translator and linguist, but also on the many experiences my friends, classmates, teachers, and colleagues have shared with me, and comments and questions I get from students at the workshops and classes I've been conducting first in Monterey, and then in Seattle since 2002 when I moved here.

The Language Realm website and its blog will serve as a way for me to offer new information as it comes along, and keep translators abreast of the industry as best as I can. You can post messages on the blog or via the website, and I will respond, either directly or with a relevant posting or article, and sometimes both. It is also a repository of useful material, including sample resumes, glossaries, and other tools and information that cannot be easily presented in book form.

Of course, all errors in this book are my own, though I have done my best to make certain there are none. I would like to thank the many teachers, students, colleagues, coworkers, and friends who helped me understand the translation industry and profession, challenged me with their questions, and as a result, helped form the content of this book. Rather than attempt to assemble a list of names of people who over the past 12 years have helped me in one way or another, I'll make it simple: thank you to all.

Please make certain that you, the reader, take advantage of the Language Realm and contact me with your questions. It is too soon to plan a second edition of this book, but I am always collecting information and presenting it in one form or another on my website, and appreciate any thoughts, observations, or suggestions.

Roger Chriss
Seattle, 2006
rbchriss@languagerealm.com
www.languagerealm.com

Overview of the Profession

The translation profession has been steadily growing for many years now, it was noted as a cool career in the book *Cool Careers for Dummies*, and the Occupational Outlook Handbook produced by the Bureau of Labor Statistics in the U.S. Department of Labor foresees faster than average increase in employment opportunities from now through 2014. Government agencies are actively recruiting translators while the media reports on shortages, and the private sector is, after recovering from the dot.com bubble and recession, is hiring actively. It is, in other words, a good time to be a translator, and a good time to enter the profession.

The translation industry in the United States is broadly speaking split into two halves: translators who are employed full-time by a company or organization, and translators who are self-employed, working on a freelance basis for various clients, either part-time or full-time. Both options are viable, and many translators work in-house for a few years before becoming freelance, though some, myself included, start out as freelance translators and remain so.

Of course, the situation is not quite that simple. Many factors are involved in becoming a translator, and that is what this book is all about. This book is based on my 14 years of experience in the industry as a freelance translator, over ten years of teaching courses and workshops on the business of translation at the Monterey Institute of International Studies and the Bellevue Community College's Translation and Interpretation Institute, my article series "Translation as a Profession," and conversations with classmates, colleagues, clients, students, and industry insiders. There is a lot to this profession, and most of it is usually hidden from view. That is where this book comes in. It is a guide, a description, and a wealth of advice and strategies for both newcomers and experienced members in the profession to advance careers, increase income, and create job stability and security.

To start we have to get the basics straight, so this chapter is devoted to describing translators, translation itself, and the industry in general. We have to lay the groundwork here and now, because the translation industry is quite different from most others, and will probably feel like unfamiliar territory without a proper introduction.

Who Is A Translator

A translator is a combination of writer and linguist, a person who takes written material such as newspaper or magazine articles, books, manuals or documents in one language and converts it into the equivalent in another language. In other words, a translator converts meaning from one language to another. By definition a translator knows two languages at or close to native proficiency, and often knows a third or even a fourth. Translators also by definition must have strong reading and writing skills, as well as a deep knowledge of the subject material they are working on.

Translators typically work into their native language, that is to say that they translate material that is in their second, acquired language into the language they were born into and educated in. There are exceptions, especially among people who are born, raised, and educated bilingually, but in general translators produce their best work when going into their mother tongue.

In the translation profession the translator's native language is referred to as the *A language* or native language, and the non-native languages as a *B language* or *C language*. A B language is one which the translator can speak, read, and write virtually as a native speaker does. A C language is one which the translator can read and understand almost like a native, but does not necessarily speak or write so well. Obviously we all have an A language, and equally evident, all translators have a B language. Many translators have more than one B language, and some also have C languages. What very few people have is two A languages, and even if you are one of those who do, take care in making the claim, as many people will be skeptical.

In practice, many organizations will only recognize one A or native language even if you can legitimately claim two. Online translation profiles now offered by many translation agencies for translators to use to register themselves to get work, and job applications at translation companies only allow one language as the A or native language. If you have two A languages, in other words you were born, raised, and educated completely bilingually, you should still claim as your A language the one you have stronger writing skills or more reading experience in. This will probably be the language you did your university-level education in or which you have worked professionally with. Then introduce your other A language, which some people would consider a very strong B language, and go from there.

Translators and the translation industry tend to avoid the word *fluency* because it creates too much confusion. It is an imprecise term in an industry that requires an exact description of a person's ability. So instead many companies and organizations follow the ILR Scale, developed by the Interagency Language Roundtable years back, and used by language teachers, the government, and private industry to rate a person's facility with a language. The ILR Scale defines four areas of proficiency: reading, writing, speaking, and listening. It then rates each from 0 (no ability at all) to 5 (completely native ability). The ILR Scale also has a translation ranking system, which works differently from the other four components of language proficiency, since a person can be a 4+ in reading, writing, speaking, and listening in their second language and have no translation ability whatsoever.

What Is A Translator

A good translator is by definition bilingual. The opposite is not necessarily true, however. A born and bred bilingual will still need two things to become a translator: first, the skills and experience necessary for translation; second, knowledge of the field in which he or she will translate. The skills and experience for translation include the ability to write well in the language the translator is working into, what is commonly called the *target language*, and the ability to read and understand the language being translated, what is known as the *source language*. Further, the bilingual who would be a translator must be able to work with the latest word processing software, machine-assisted translation tools, and typical Internet and email applications.

So does a born and bred bilingual makes a better translator than someone who learned the B language later in life? There is no definite answer, but the following issues are important. First, a born and bred bilingual often does not know any language well enough to translate, with some even suffering from what is known as alingualism, a state in which a person lacks a full, fluent command of any language. Second, born and bred bilinguals often don not know the culture of either of their languages well enough to provide good translations, or cannot recognize what aspects of the source language and its culture need to be treated with particular care, as they are in a sense too close to the language. And last, they often lack the analytical linguistic skills developed through conscious study of a language and necessary to work through a text.

On the other hand, the acquired bilingual may not have the same in-depth knowledge of colloquialisms, slang, and dialect that the born bilingual has. As well, the acquired bilingual will not be able to translate as readily in both directions (from the B to A language and the A to B language). Finally, born bilinguals often have a greater appreciation of the subtleties and nuances of both their languages than someone who learns their B language later in life can ever hope to have.

Where Do Translators Come From

Translators come from all backgrounds. Some have graduate degrees, as offered at the Monterey Institute of International Studies or Kent State University, some have undergraduate degrees as are now available at several schools in the United States, and some have certificates in translation as can be earned at programs such as Miami Dade, NYU, or Bellevue Community College's Translation & Interpretation Institute. There are equivalent opportunities in Europe, with excellent schools in London, Paris, and Geneva, and in Asia, where Japan has Simul Academy in Tokyo. Also, many translators have undergraduate or graduate degrees, or at least coursework, in their languages, or the literature or history related to their language.

While a specialized degree in translation is useful, it is far from necessary. What counts more than anything else is ability. The translation profession is open to all entrants. There is currently no required accreditation or certification exam, no required academic background or particular degree, and only general expectations for how you learned your languages. So while there are no barriers to entry, there is one essential requirement: you must be able to translate. The profession is not especially tolerant or forgiving. Ability counts for everything.

So where does this ability come from? It starts with Nature, of course. Some people can just translate, and become outstanding translators with little training or experience, and other people simply cannot translate, even after many years of training and experience. But most people lie between these two extremes, in other words, though inherent ability is important, Nurture helps immensely. Most translators are very well read in their languages, and have thoroughly developed their writing skills. Some are writers who use translation as a way to write for a living. Others are fascinated by language and use translation as a way to be close to their favorite subject. Still others are experts in certain fields and use their language skills to work in that field. But regardless, they have the language skills to translate.

Almost all professional translators in the United States have at a minimum a college degree. This has become a default requirement with virtually no exceptions. I personally have met one in the past ten years, and he was a former U.S. Marine trained in Arabic at the Defense Language Institute (DLI) in the late 1980s, then served as a translator during the first Gulf War, and found himself back in the profession after 9/11. So although it is possible to enter and succeed in the profession without a Bachelor's degree, you are much better off getting one if you don't already have one.

Some translators also have advanced degrees, either in translation or in the field they specialize in, and a few even have both. Most translators have university-level language training in their second language, and may have taken writing classes for their native language. Some started language study earlier, others later, but very few translators have no language training at all. The analytical skills learned in the classroom are very useful when translating, and seem to be all but essential to developing strong translation skills.

Translators have spent time, usually years, living in the countries where their languages are spoken. I know of translators who have spent seven or even ten years in the countries of their B language. Some translators have spent more time in the country of their B language than in the country of their A language. The notable exception to this general rule is Spanish in the United States and English abroad. Because Spanish is used so widely and is as common as English in many parts of the U.S., some translators learn and then work in the language without ever leaving the U.S. As well, translators in other countries often work from English into their native language with just the language training they received in school and the regular exposure to U.S. media and culture.

Translators have to be analytical. They must develop the skills, through classroom training or experience, to dissect language for the purpose of extracting meaning and then representing that meaning in another language. Translators do not work word by word; rather they identify a meaning unit in the source language, sometimes through a non-conscious, apparently intuitive process, and then reproduce that meaning unit in the target language while making certain that terminology is correct, the style of the original is preserved, and the result sounds natural.

Above all, translators must have a deep interest and dedication to the languages they work with. This leads to what I call the maintenance problem. As any native speaker of English who has lived abroad knows, your English skills deteriorate while outside the U.S. When I came back to the United States after two years in Japan, where I hardly ever spoke, heard, or read English, I found watching the evening news difficult because the speech was too fast, and I read noticeably slowly compared to my friends. This of course faded within a month. But if you are a translator, you have to maintain your skills in all of your working languages, and so must listen, read, speak, and write on a regular basis. I watch hours of news and other programming in Japanese (my B language) every week, and regularly read articles and books in it, too. The Internet and cable television make maintaining one's language skills easier than ever, but you still have to make the effort.

Translators as Experts

The knowledge of the field the translator is working in is often overlooked by translators and those that hire them. Translators are by definition language professionals, but they also have to cultivate knowledge of the areas they work in. Few translators claim to be able to translate anything written in their languages; this would imply that you are an expert on everything. A translator who says he can translate anything is a jack of all trades and a master of none. Clients and employers will not feel confident working with such a translator. Further, subject matter has become so specialized that most translators have to work within one or a few related areas, for instance legal, financial, medical, computers, or electrical engineering, to name a few. Each field has its own vocabulary, syntax, and style; the translator has to work hard to develop the knowledge necessary to deal with such material.

The knowledge also includes two other important factors. First, the translator should have the background knowledge to work in the field. This does not mean that a medical translator should have an M.D., or that a translator of semiconductor documents should be an electrical engineer. But some background, experience, or education is essential. This can be obtained through coursework, on-the-job experience, or self-study. No one seems too concerned with exactly how translators develop their subject knowledge, unless that knowledge is very arcane or exotic. Claiming that you acquired a thorough knowledge of quantum field theory without ever having taken a single relevant course would be difficult to accept (and if you did, you should probably be a physicist). You will have to back up any claim of expertise you make by doing the translation, and the profession can be harsh if your work is poor. In other words, you must have the specialized knowledge. And though some translators do have undergraduate or even graduate degrees in their areas of specialization, most do not.

Second, the translator should have the necessary resources to deal with the material they translate. This means dictionaries, glossaries, and any other terminology, language, or subject matter resources. Such resources can include Web sites devoted to translation or terminology, discussion groups concerning translation or language, friends or colleagues who work in the profession, and magazines and journals. And translators have to work tirelessly to keep current with the fields they work in by reading related material. They also have to invest the time and money in maintaining their reference library and taking courses or acquiring good textbooks.

In my case, I routinely take computer and engineering courses through extension programs, improving my knowledge base and keeping current with the latest technologies. For instance, I started learning about IPv6 a few years back, and am glad I did because it is now appearing in material I work on. I also routinely check out textbooks and reference books from my local library, browse the sections I'm not familiar or comfortable with, and review material I think I know. When possible, I do this in all my languages.

In other words, professional translators are always learning. Becoming a translator is a lengthy process, and being a translator is also a process, not a state. You don't just acquire a language in a few weeks or months from a book and then begin translating.

Heinrich Schliemann may have learned to read each of his languages in six weeks, but he couldn't write or speak them (nor did he need to). Moreover, at that time, languages had considerably more limited vocabularies than now. Most of all, reading and translating are two completely separate activities.

So at what point are you ready to begin translating? Simple: When you feel that your abilities of expression and comprehension in your A and B languages are strong enough that you can do the job properly by the client's deadline. The length of time to cultivate these abilities depends on the person and the language. Native speakers of English have an easier time with the Romance and Germanic languages because their grammars, syntax, and vocabulary are relatively familiar. A language like Chinese or Japanese takes a long time simply because you have to learn to read and understand thousands of characters, as well as deal with grammar, syntax, and structure wholly unrelated to what is found in English.

Your feelings about your ability may not be the best way to decide when you are ready to translate. Remember, the profession can be quite unforgiving, so you want your entrance to be successful. Taking courses, earning a degree or certificate, or passing a certification exam such as the one offered by the American Translators' Association are ways to test your ability and acquire proof that you can translate. Experience living or studying in the country of your B language is another form of proof. Mentoring programs and related work experience are yet another. Whatever you do, make certain that you verify your sense of your ability.

What Is a Translation

A turn-of-the-century Russian translator said: "Translation is like a woman, if she is beautiful, she is not faithful; if she is faithful, she is not beautiful." Setting aside for the moment the blatant sexism in this quote, we can see one of the core challenges in translation. Translators must strike a balance between fidelity to the source text and readability in the target language. We have all seen material that is so obviously translated as to sound awkward in our native languages, and in some cases as to bear enough hallmarks of the source language as to be readily identifiable as coming from it. The best translation is the one that no one recognizes as a translation. In other words, the document should read as though it were written in the target language originally. This implies, by extension, that the translator's effort is transparent, and the translator ends up being invisible. In other words, you have done outstanding work when no one realizes you have done anything.

Achieving this level of translation is challenging, to say the least. It takes years of practice for most people, and many never achieve it. Fortunately, the industry is not often interested in having translations that are that good, largely because they take too long to produce. Your employer or client decides what level of quality is needed, since they have to live with the results of your work. You may, especially if you are a freelance translator, have to patiently explain to them the options they have, how long each might take, and how much each possible version will cost. They'll decide if they want a literal, if unreadable, translation or if they want a Pulitzer Prize-winning text.

If your client can't decide, doesn't know, or won't tell you, then strike a balance. This is easier with some languages and some subject areas than others. Although most people think that technical material is easiest for stylistic considerations, consider this. Academic style varies from nation to nation and culture to culture. For instance, in English, we generally present our thesis, then give the evidence, develop the argument, and then reach the conclusion. However, in Japanese, we usually present a general idea, give the evidence slowly with lots of discussion, and then reach some tentative statement about the idea in the form of a conclusion. Other differences exist among other language pairs. Somehow you have to deal with these differences.

Another potential pitfall with technical translation is that often the client cannot let you see or touch the object in question. If you are translating a computer system manual, it is very helpful to see and even work a little with the system. The same holds for a video game, home audio component, or for that matter a scanning electron microscope, which I realize is hardly something you want in your home, but I have translated manuals and technical specifications for such technology. Sometimes seeing the product in question is not possible, the system or software may still be in development. You might have to create terminology for the system, only to find that the client wants something else. You then have to go back and change everything.

Every form of translation has its challenges and problems. Even seemingly simple assignments, such as translating a business card, can present difficulties in some language combinations. Japanese names are notoriously difficult to figure out how to pronounce; often the only reliable solution, even for Japanese people themselves, is to ask the person. Spanish names are famous for their length, and often should be shortened when rendered into English.

The most difficult problem is when you encounter something in one language that doesn't exist in the other. Financial instruments, legal procedures, and government and business structures vary from nation to nation and culture to culture. Although standard glossaries exist for the most commonplace of these, in other words those that you might hear about in a major newspaper or magazine, translators are usually dealing with new or specialized material and information, so you might be stuck having to christen something on your own, or leave it in the A language and put in a translator's note explaining what the term means.

What Is Translated

Most of the material people want translated is not high culture. I have translated materials ranging from articles in medical journals on deep vein thrombosis to bearer's bonds, from family registers (the Japanese equivalent of a birth certificate) and university transcripts to engineering specifications for DVDs or toilet manufacturing processes. The longest translation project I ever did was a 65,000-word book; the shortest, a two-word phrase.

Outsiders to the profession generally see translation as a slow and expensive process which most businesses and organizations would rather avoid. They prefer not to go through the hassle of calling a translation company, sending over the material, waiting for a bid, bargaining and haggling over price and form and date of delivery, and then waiting to see if they get something they can use.

Very little of what businesses do is translated. So what they do translate has to be important to someone somewhere. Therefore, it has to be important to you to do it right, especially if you want to get more work from that client or keep your job with your employer. What might seem trivial to you could be worth a lot to someone. I've translated lost traveler's checks surveys, interoffice memos, and advertising copy for car care products. None of this is high culture. But someone wanted it, so I did my absolute best. Remember, the only way to survive as a translator is to do a good job. You will be judged primarily if not solely by your work.

That said, materials to be translated come in all sizes and shapes. Often you have to deal with hand-written material. Someone scrawled out some message to someone else and this twenty-five-word chit of paper is now Exhibit A in an international patent infringement lawsuit. You probably won't know that, but it could happen. When I was working in-house as a translator for the City of Kawasaki in Japan, my supervisor plopped a short letter on my desk and I translated it. I later found out that Prime Minister Takeshita took this letter to President Reagan during the Summit meeting in 1988. You never know, so always be prepared and do your best.

When translating, no problem is too small, no term too minor to be ignored. The people who read your translation don't know the source language. If they did, they wouldn't have hired you. It's easy to see why an article describing a surgical procedure must be done very accurately. It might be harder to see why the comments of a Japanese teenager on an airline survey would be important, but they could affect future policy of that carrier. You have to take it all seriously if you want to be taken seriously as a translator.

The Role of the Translator

Translators are language professionals. They are applied linguists, competent writers, diplomats, and educated amateurs. Like linguists, translators have to be capable of analyzing the syntax and structures of their languages, researching terminology and colloquialisms, and handling new developments in their languages. Like writers, translators have to be accustomed to working long hours alone on a subject which interests few people and with a language that few people around them know. Like diplomats, translators have to be sensitive to the cultural and social differences which exist in their languages and be capable of addressing these issues when translating. And like educated amateurs, translators have to know the basics and some of the details about the subjects they deal with.

The above is an idealization of the translator, an image which professional translators aspire to and achieve with varying degrees of success. Not all translators need to overflow with these qualities. They must, however, have them in sufficient measure to be able to translate their material in a manner acceptable to their employer or clients.

Somewhere in the process of translating, the translator will come across all these issues. When I work with technical or medical documents, I have to deal with the intricacies of technical writing in Japanese and English and research new or obscure terms (and sometimes invent my own). I struggle with my English to polish and hone it so that the client sees the material as natural, without the tell-tale signs that it was translated from Japanese. I have to research the subject matter using authoritative sources, expert associates, and current articles or books. Finally, I deal with the differences between Japanese and American culture, in particular when negotiating with clients or translating material with significant cultural content.

The fundamental rule when you're not sure of something in your source text, the material that is to be translated, is to ask. When you have doubts or questions, call the client or contact your project manager or supervisor, ask your question, and then get the answer. If you're still not sure, make a note of it in the final translation. Such translator's notes are well-tolerated, and sometimes even expected. I've heard that clients are at times suspicious when they don't see these notes. After all, how much can a translator know about new surgical procedures to clear a pulmonary embolism?

In-House Versus Freelance

Translators either work for themselves as independent contractors or for the translation department of a company or organization, or for translation agencies or companies. The former are typically called freelance translators, or freelancers, and the latter, in-house translators.

If you are just entering the profession, or if you are considering translation as a career, you have to look closely at these two options to decide which is right for you. Although both involve translation itself, each also involves certain personality traits and individual characteristics. In addition, there are implications for the kind of work you will do, the technology you will use to do your work, and who you will work with.

As a freelance translator, you are a business owner. You will take care of marketing, invoicing, accounts payable and receivable, taxes, equipment purchases and maintenance, and medical and retirement benefits. Freelance translators may make more per year on average than in-house translators, but their income is far more variable, and they have to cover all their own expenses, including all taxes, retirement funds, medical and other forms of insurance, and business and operating costs.

As an in-house translator, you work for someone else. You go to your office in the morning, sit in your cubicle during the day translating whatever the company or organization needs, attend meetings to discuss large-scale translation projects, terminology, or equipment, go to training sessions to learn to use the new LAN system or MAT software, and then go home in the evening. Like most jobs, you get paid vacation, insurance, half of your Social Security and FICA taxes paid, and the other benefits that come with employment.

Although the remaining chapters will discuss the above differences between freelance and in-house translation in detail, and even offer suggestions as to which people might be suited for, I will say here that often careful consideration of your personality and working style are unnecessary. The reason is money. Only if you are financially and personally in a position to assume the risks of starting a business, should you then look closely at your personal strengths and preferences to see if you will be comfortable as an independent contractor. Furthermore, some languages offer more freelance work, while others offer more in-house work. For instance, since the start of the War on Terror in the U.S., the military and intelligence community have been hiring translators of Arabic, Korean, Farsi, and Davi among others, regularly. It is highly unlikely that a freelance Davi translator could make a significant amount of money.

So before you figure out which you might prefer, consider the financial and business realities of the languages you know. To start as a freelance translator, you will need a several thousand dollars to get the computer hardware and software you need, to do some marketing, and to wait out the first few months during which time you will likely have little work, and you will be patiently waiting for that first invoice to be paid. It may take several years for your work flow to stabilize at a level you are comfortable with. So if you are single with few financial responsibilities, some money saved, and don't mind the risk, the answer to the money question is affirmative: you can have a go at freelance translation. If however you are married with a couple of children, have the usual expenses of a mortgage, medical costs, and so forth, then you should think very carefully before starting up as a freelance translator.

There is also a strong argument for getting your feet wet in the industry by working for someone else. You can think of it as paid on-the-job training. You will learn more about translation by translating than any other way. And you will also acquire not only all that secondary know-how, such as word processing, negotiating, or filing tax forms, but also lots of practical knowledge about the industry, such as word rates, which language pairs or subject areas are in demand, or what technologies are likely to affect translation in the near future. You might even develop relationships that can be turned into clients for a freelance business. So consider starting off as an in-house translator, especially if you are uncomfortable with the financial aspects of working for yourself, have a language pair that is unlikely to yield a good freelance income, or are uncertain as to how you will feel about working at home alone.

A Good Translator

The very qualities that seem to make a good translator, those of attention to detail, passion for languages and research, care and craft in writing, also seem to be those that make a poor negotiator or marketing person. How does one overcome this paradox? One, force yourself to market, even when you don't want to. Make a commitment to yourself to send find and contact 100 potential clients this month; to call or email your top five clients for a brief exchange of information; to submit a tax return on or before April 15, and your quarterly taxes on time. You are in business; as Donald Trump suggests, treat your business like a lover, with the passion and commitment necessary to make it thrive.

You should also show your clients that you are a business professional. Translators want to be treated as professionals, and therefore, they have to behave as professionals. Take the time to learn about your industry, about your languages, about your subject specializations, and about the technology you use to do the work you do. In any industry, there are always too many people wanting to do the work to be done, and too few people who can actually do the work properly. As a translator, you want to make clear to everyone that you are in the latter category, that you can do the work.

Above all, as a translator, you are standing between two people or organizations, one which created the material and the other which wants to read it. You are their solution to this otherwise intractable problem. Remember, it's the information age, and there's lots of information out there in lots of languages. Translators bring this precious commodity to the people who want it.

Translation Life

U nless you are a translator or know someone who is, exactly what a translator does may be a bit of a mystery. I don't mean the inner workings of a translator's brain as the translation process proceeds, but rather what a day in the life of a translator is like. There are no television shows or movies that portray translators at work, and few internships available. But if you want to make the most of a career in translation, you need to know what's what.

As explained in the previous chapter, translators either work for organizations or themselves. The working life of each is quite different, and knowing about both can help you decide which way you want to go. Further, many people who work for themselves as translators do so on a part-time basis. The Bureau of Labor Statistics' Occupational Outlook Handbook reports that about 15% of translators are self-employed, but then admits that this number is likely higher. It is probably a lot higher because of how many freelance translators only work part-time. Some do so by choice, others because they haven't yet built up a full client base. And some in-house translators even freelance at night or on the weekends to increase their income, or pave the way for a transition to being fully self-employed.

Further complicating the picture is the reality that many in-house translators are actually playing several roles in the company. One friend of mine who has graduate degrees in translation and accounting has found herself performing both tasks for companies she's worked for. Another translator I know developed such strong website design and management skills that half of his day was spent working with HTML and other web technologies. And yet another translator, this time with strong project management skills, ended up becoming the lead translator of his team, dividing his time between translating, managing the team's translation projects, working with external vendors to handle projects his team couldn't, and even hiring and training translators. So the in-house world can be quite varied. By contrast, the world of a freelance translator is much more straightforward, so we'll start there.

A Day in My Life as a Translator

Since I've been working full-time as a freelance translator for 14 years, I've know well how I work, and have developed a variety of strategies and techniques for getting my translations done on time, and taking care of all the rest of what is involved in running a business. So read along as I describe a typical working day.

I start my work day around 7:30 A.M., in part because I live and work in Washington State but have clients on the East Coast who may need my attention before midday, and in part because by starting early I am assured an hour of two of considerable quiet during which I can work at full concentration and without distraction.

First I review any new email or files that need my attention, answering client queries and making sure I am on schedule for my current projects. Then I translate. I find translation to require consider-able concentration, particularly if I am working on a document with sticky syntax or troublesome terminology, with concepts that are new or unfamiliar, or with printing of such poor quality that the job turns into an exercise in archaeological decipherment. Phone calls and email can interrupt the flow I get into once I start on a text, so by starting early I all but guarantee myself a couple of hours in which, except for rare cases, I can crank along at a steady, productive pace.

Also, there is some evidence from neurology and cognitive science that the language function of the brain operates best in the morning hours. Whether or not this has any impact on translation remains to be seen, but I do find that I work better, producing higher quality text in less time, in the morning.

I do sometimes get calls early in the morning, occasionally as early as 2:00 or 3:00 am, though that hasn't happened much since the industry shifted to email-based communication. Since freelance translators inevitably work for businesses that are many time zones ahead or behind them, sometimes even a day ahead if the International Date Line is involved, calls can in theory come at virtually any time or the day or night. As such, some businesses may come to expect their freelancer to be on call 24 hours a day, not only able to accept faxes or email, a relatively automatic process, but to confirm on the telephone receipt of such faxes or email, and even to discuss a project, if not actually work on it. I've gotten calls from New York at 9:00 pm Pacific time on a Friday night. Ignoring the obvious question for such callers, I cannot support the practice of 24/7 availability. Further, if you want to do business with someone, or if you want a favor from someone, you really ought to call when it is convenient for that person, and not for you. A few people have called me at 1:00 or 2:00 a.m.; I do not answer the phone at that hour unless I see a caller ID from a close family member or friend, and I'm disinclined to call back such people.

Translators have to be willing to work hard for their clients, but as independent contractors they also have to protect their life outside of work and discourage clients from thinking of them as always available. Whether you choose to be available for your clients at all times or to ignore your business phone, fax, and email at certain times is up to you, but I strongly suggest the latter so as to prevent excess stress (will they never leave me alone!?), job dissatisfaction (all I do is work, work, work!), and burn out (I can't take it any more). A career is like a marathon: only by pacing yourself will you be able to retire with grace and poise.

If, by the way, you are awoken by your business phone very early in the morning, don't answer it. Save yourself the embarrassment and confusion. You will not, regardless of how quickly you think you wake up, sound particularly coherent or give intelligent answers to questions. Let your answering machine take the call, then call the client back once you are fully awake and aware, ready to work. Also, there's nothing wrong with firmly yet gracefully insisting that clients call you during your normal business hours.

The rest of my day can unfold in one of a few ways, depending on how much work I have and when the work has to be done, along with any other business-related matters that I have to attend to.

On days when I have a lot of work, I spend the rest of the day working on the translation until either it is done, or at least far enough along. Whenever I receive an assignment, I check the length of the source text, do a quick calculation, and figure out how many words I have to do every day. I then do a little more than that per day.

As I translate, when I find words or phrases I don't know, I note them on a separate page and then look them up later. Sometimes, my search for these words takes me to a library, sifting through dictionaries, encyclopedias, almanacs, and maps, or has me on the phone, checking with someone who can either tell me the word, or at least explain the concept to me. At other times, I wander the Web, looking for authoritative references from good glossary sites, since what I need is a credible source and not a random mention of the term.

On days when I have only a little work, I still begin the day by translating. Once finished with the day's quota, I work on finding more work and keeping my skills sharp. This means making certain my information with potential clients is current and available, looking for potential new clients and letting them know I exist, and studying my languages and subject areas. I watch hours of television news in Japanese per week, along with other programming. I regularly read books and articles in Japanese and English on both general subjects and the areas I translate in.

At regular intervals I also perform maintenance on my computer systems, including full scans for viruses and other malware, and complete backups of all files. I check for patches and updates to the software I use, and make sure that I have a good stock of printer ink, paper, and other office necessities. I maintain a list of things that I am running out of on an index card in a drawer, and then when I am next at Costco or a similar superstore, I stock up. I don't like to shop, so I tend to have a good stockpile of material, but of course it gets used up sooner or later.

I also have to deal with the financial side of my business, keeping track of which clients have paid me, what invoices are pending, and if any invoices are late. This means I check my bookkeeping records, which I maintain in a database I built. It will automatically alert me to when an invoice is late and offer to print a late notice. If you don't want to build such a tool yourself, there are several good software packages available for small-business owners, in particular QuickBooks.

Then there's the logistical side of my business. I have to retain copies of old translations, old invoices, financial and tax materials, along with receipts for business purchases. Eventually the time limit for doing this expires, and so the oldest material gets shredded and dumped in a recycling bin. I do this about twice a year, usually on a weekend when I' not otherwise occupied.

Finally, I have to from time to time deal with equipment purchases. Every few years something needs to be replaced. Office chairs wear out and become uncomfortable to sit on; the printer ceases to print, or does so with such noise and reluctance that a new one is in order. As a self-employed translator, this too is my responsibility, so I go online, check web sites like Cnet.com and *PC*

Magazine's site (pcmagazine.com) for reviews for computer equipment and make the best choice I can. For office furniture, I visit the obvious stores and choose something comfortable and reasonably priced.

If I don't have any work, I work on finding work. Despite well over a decade in the translation profession, I still have the occasional day when I don't have anything on my desk to translate. Freelance translators, like most self-employed people, generally describe their work flow as being "feast or famine." You are either drowning in work, translating from dawn until late at night, trying to meet your impossible deadlines and fretting over carpal tunnel syndrome as you do so, or you are waiting by the phone, praying to the patron saint of translators, St. Jerome, or perhaps the patron saint of lost causes. This feast or famine cycle has become more accentuated in recent years as clients have shortened the time frame for translation projects. A job that might have been granted a week five years ago is now given only three or four days. So expect to work very hard when you have work, and then have down time during which you have to look for more work.

You probably noted a paradox here. When translators have lots of work, they have virtually no time to market themselves for the upcoming and inevitable dry spell. When they have no work, it is too late to do the necessary marketing. A freelance translator is in the business of providing translation services, which means that you are more than a translator; you are a businessperson, whose duties include finding work.

For now, remember this truism for translators and all other freelancers: market always! In the chapter on marketing, we'll discuss a wide variety of strategies and tricks for finding clients if you are or want to be a freelance translator, or finding an employer if you are or want to be an in-house translator.

Income

Income in translation, particularly freelance translation, varies considerably. At the lower end, a freelance translator can have negative income, a result of spending more to run your business than you earn from it in a given year. The upper end of the range is filled with rumors, from stories of individuals earning over

$150,000 per year to claims by duos or small teams of generating in excess of $200,000 per year.

Realistically, few translators ever have negative income, except perhaps during their first year of business. This is most likely to happen if this first business year consists of the last two months of the calendar year, during which considerable funds are spent on computers and other office essentials. Also, few translators ever make over $60,000 per year, and you should be very skeptical of claims of income above $75,000. Of course, there are exceptions, but for the most part translators can expect to make between $35,000 and $45,000 per year. according to Salary.com, which has statistics for a tremendous variety of jobs nationwide. Their numbers are consistent with the Occupational Outlook Handbook, top. If you hear stories about income levels much higher than that, just smile and bear in mind that most people exaggerate their income, at least to some extent.

The American Translators Association publishes annually the results of their income survey of their members. In 2006, the survey, based on data collected the previous year, reported that full-time translators had income as follows:

- In-house private sector: $58,147
- Independent contractor: $54,207
- Government translator: $54,305

These are nice numbers, and certainly inspiring for newcomers to the profession. But a little explanation is in order before you get too excited. First, the ATA survey covers only ATA members. In the survey above, more than half the respondents had graduate degrees, more than half had been in the profession for over 10 years, and about two-thirds were born outside the U.S.

By contrast, Salary.com gives the following numbers for full-time translators, in-house and freelance combined:

- Median income: $40,522
- Highest 25%: $49,536
- Lowest 25%: $33,985

These numbers are similar to Department of Labor's Occupational Outlook Handbook, which gives hourly rates instead of annual income:

- $16.28 in May, 2004
- $9.67 for the lowest 10%
- $27.45 for the highest 10%

The handbook also notes that earnings vary depending on language, subject matter, skill, experience, education, and market demand. Further, it states: "Individuals classified as language specialists for the Federal Government earned an average of $71,625 annually in 2005. Limited information suggests that some highly skilled interpreters and translators—for example, high-level conference interpreters—working full time can earn more than $100,000 annually."

So why the discrepancies between the ATA's report and two other reliable sources? First, the ATA's survey relies on self-reporting. You fill in the numbers for your income yourself, with no independent verification of those numbers. Since people tend to exaggerate their income, this may explain some of the difference. The rest is simply the result of the ATA's survey population. The respondents were all highly educated and very experienced, and naturally would be earning above-average incomes within the translation profession.

In other words, use the ATA's numbers as representative of what your potential income will be once you've amassed experience and credentials, and use the Salary.com numbers to get an idea of where you're likely to start. As in all professions, starting income tends to be lower than you might like, and lots of work goes into reaching the higher income levels.

Income Trends

Rates and income for translators have been soft for the past five years, falling even for some language pairs, Spanish in particular. So you don't need to find the most current information to get a realistic picture of your income prospects. Broadly speaking, freelancers, who in the United States are almost always paid by the word, working with European languages are seeing rates on the order of $0.08 to $0.12 per word at most, and freelancers working with Asian or other rare languages are getting roughly $0.09 to $0.15 per word. In-house translators are still starting around or a little above $33,000, with the average near $40,000, and a few exceeding $50,000 after years of experience. These freelance rates do vary by subject area and job schedule; the in-house salaries vary depending on education, experience, language, and subject area.

So if you are asked if you make a lot of money as a translator, your answer will probably be no, though that does depend on what you consider a lot of money. And it also depends on what month or year you are in, as translation, like all businesses, is not perfectly stable or predictable.

Income for a freelance translator can be calculated with a simple equation:

$$Income = Average\ Word\ Rate \times Words\ Translated$$

Figure out how many words you translate per week and the average word rate for the projects those words are a part of, and the result is your income for that week. Similarly, you can calculate your monthly income or your annual income. If you are getting $0.09 per word (a reasonable rate for the market overall) and translating 2000 words a day, five days a week, fifty weeks per year (we'll assume you take a vacation day here and there, celebrate the usual holidays, and get sick once in a while), then your income for the year is $45,000. Of course it may make a year or more to find a steady flow of work at that rate and learn to translate that many words per day every day, but this is a reasonable model that many people do achieve.

Translation Riches

So what about the rumors of translation riches? What about the Web sites offering systems to earn high five-digit or even six-figure incomes? First of all: caveat lector. Don't believe everything you read, especially if it's marketing material, and in particular if it's on the Web. Ask yourself why such people aren't using their own system rather than trying to sell it? Ask yourself how many translators have been featured on *Lifestyles of the Rich and Famous*? Do the members of your local translators' group arrive in Rolls Royces, do the experienced translators at the annual ATA Conference fly in on their own Lear jets, do you know any translators who have retired early from their translation earnings?

But let's approach this differently. What would it take to earn $150,000 per year as a freelance translator? Simple math shows that at $0.10 per word (a reasonable rate) you'd have to do 5,000 words per day, six days a week, 52 weeks per year, to earn $156,000 annually. Or at a rate of $0.20 per word, you'd have to do 2,500 words per day.

To get $0.20 per word, you'd have to find all your own clients, since no agency is going to pay you $0.20 per word except under extremely extenuating circumstances that could not possibly continue for a year's time. Even direct clients rarely pay that much these days, unless you are providing desktop publishing and other ancillary services, which themselves can take a lot of time and require expensive software and other technology. And direct clients generally expect a completed translation, one that has been edited, proofread, and perhaps even prepared for printing. So you either have to do all of that yourself, or you have to pay someone else to do it. Either way, your overall income will fall.

Second, you'd have to be very fast and efficient to maintain that level of productivity over a year's time. There are people who do it. There are even people who claim to do in excess of 7,000 words per day regularly, some of whom simply dictate their translation into a tape recorder, and then pay others to transcribe and edit their work. I'm very skeptical of such claims, since most translators report that after 2,500 to 3,000 words per day their brains are fried.

Third, you'd spend a great deal of your time working, probably in excess of ninety hours per week. Remember that for every hour of translation you do, you will likely have five to ten minutes worth of other office work, including marketing, invoicing, accounts receivable and payable, banking, purchasing office supplies and equipment, maintaining and upgrading your computer system, evaluating and acquiring new dictionaries and other language resources, and doing taxes, to name a few possibilities. This is a part of running a business, and you can certainly pay other people to do this work for you, but again, what you pay others comes out of your income.

So set aside the myth of rapid riches. Starting freelance translators with good skills and languages that are in demand in the market can reasonably expect to make $30,000 in their first or second year, perhaps more, sometimes even considerably more, depending on their language combination and subject specialization. The average in the industry seems to be around $40,000 per year, with a few people making in excess of $100,000 per year. But those that do so rarely have time for little else but eating and sleeping. There are far easier, faster, and more pleasant ways to get rich. With the right education, such as in international law or finance, and a few languages, one can go very far and very high in industry, or so I'm told. In other words, translation is not a way to get rich quickly or make it into the Forbes' 400.

For those of you that dream of translating a great novel or book and living off the royalties, doing so will be extraordinarily difficult. Authors generally get about 10% of the hardback sales and 4% or the paperback sales in royalties and have to fight very hard for that. They're not going to yield part of it to some translator unless they absolutely have to. I've translated books and gotten paid the same way I did for everything else: by the word. The translators of the *Harry Potter* novels are paid by the word. Many years ago, different relations existed between publishers and translators, but nowadays, the only advantage to translating a book is that you have a lot of work for a long time. Also, royalty payments generally are paid starting six to twelve months after the book hits the bookstores, which will likely be six to twelve months after you finish translating it. That is too long to wait for a substantial amount of income, though this may be offset by an advance from the publisher, should you be able to get one. In sum, translating books can be a fascinating process, but approach it as a business proposition. Do the math if you are offered multiple payment options and make a strategic business and financial decision about the job.

If you're thinking of translating literature, think twice. It takes a long time to translate a work of art, and even more for it to be published. You might get some kind of royalty out of it, but hardly enough to justify the time and effort you'll expend cultivating the necessary relations with the publishers, editors, and of course, the writer (if alive). You really need to love literature if you want to do this. It can be very rewarding, I say so having done a bit of that work myself, but it is also quite demanding. Enter into such projects slowly and carefully, if at all.

So if you think $35,000 to $45,000 a year is enough to live on, to raise your family, and to prepare for retirement, then you'll be fine financially in translation. Of course, there is the theoretical maximum, and you can increase your income by finding your own clients, or providing other services. However, your income will vary from month to month and year to year. Translation is a very fickle industry, subject to the vagaries of politics and economics like few other professions are. The dot-com crash ended a five-year boom for localization that kept many translators employed and happy. The advent of the War on Terror created a demand in the U.S. intelligence community for languages that most people had not previously heard of. And the Internet has enabled offshoring of languages, particularly through Web-based services like Proz.com and TranslatorsCafe.com, that has left U.S.-based translators in some language pairs struggling.

Income for the Self-Employed

Income for in-house translators is simple: you get your paycheck less the usual deductions, and you get a raise as defined by your company. For independent contractors, your income in one year is not necessarily a good indication of your income for the next year. In fact, it is no indication at all, unless you are so well established and work in such an esoteric (but still in high demand) field that you can somehow count on work always. Furthermore, your income from month to month fluctuates. While you will never make so little as to have to choose between feeding yourself or your cat, you may well have little left over after basic expenses in some months. Other months will leave you with enough to take a luxurious vacation, though you should save at least some of that extra income in preparation for the months with less income.

Furthermore, there are financial implications of being self-employed. The details are complex and vary year to year, so what follows is necessarily general in nature. However, keep all this in mind, and keep track of all this, because it is not only important, but it's the law. And consult with a tax professional for answers to any detailed or unusual questions.

Freelance translators are self-employed, meaning that they have to file a Schedule C at the end of the tax year. They also have to pay quarterly estimated income tax (both federal and state, unless your state does not have a state income tax). And they have to pay self-employment tax, though one-half of that amount is deductible from your overall income tax.

Unfortunately, there's more. Freelance translators also have to pay all their Social Security tax, all their FICA tax, and any other taxes your state and the federal government invent in the future. Freelancers also have to fund their own retirement plans, though this does have some advantages, including more control over how your retirement funds are invested and higher ceilings for annual investment in retirement funds. And self-employed people need to arrange for their own health coverage and life insurance, both of which tend to cost progressively more per year as one ages. Some freelancers of course receive benefits from a spouse or domestic partner, but often at a price, and many receive no such benefits at all. Overall, freelancers end up paying a lot more in tax than someone who works for someone else.

However, you can take many more deductions than people who are regular employees can. First and foremost is the well-known "Business Use of Home" deduction. You can also deduct as expenses any and all equipment, tools, and supplies, including computer hardware and software, paper, stamps, envelopes, paper clips, erasers, and dictionaries that you use, as well as a percent of your telephone and utility bills, and a part of your medical insurance costs (this percentage changes almost every year). Furthermore, you can deduct advertising costs, finance charges for business stuff bought with a credit card, and cost of membership to professional associations and subscriptions to professional journals and magazines. The details of income, finances, and taxes are covered in a separate chapter, so don't worry if it's not all clear yet.

In sum, if you can handle variety and unpredictability in your income as well as the responsibility of managing your personal and business finances, then being a self-employed won't be a problem. If you want a paycheck every month with the same amount on it, and you want to see that amount go up incrementally over the years, then look for an in-house position.

How to Survive

There seem to be two fundamental rules in the translation profession. Most successful translators seem to follow both, though some successful translators follow neither.

> Rule Number One: Work in the country of your B language.
> Rule Number Two: Marry a native speaker of your B language.

These rules are not meant to be humorous. Translators typically do make ten to twenty percent more working into a foreign language in the United States as compared to translating into English. And some agencies and employers are more comfortable giving work to a translator whose spouse is a native speaker of the translator's B language. I've had a few agencies choose not to give me work because I was not married to a Japanese woman. Obviously these rules are not meant to suggest that those who break them are doomed to failure, but those who do will have to work harder. I am one such example, living in the U.S. with English as my native language and never having been married to a Japanese woman. By any measure I am successful, so it can be done. But it is also harder.

Now then, what to do when there isn't much work coming in? One possibility is to rely on your spouse's income (not feasible unless you are married). Another possibility is rely on the money you have in your bank account (assumes you have enough money). A third possibility is to do something else part-time.

Many translators also do other things on the side. I personally consider myself a consultant who provides language services to anyone who wants them. I have taught English, Japanese, and Spanish over the years. I have done copy editing, proofreading, and written abstracts and text analyses for people. I have worked part-time as a desktop publisher and a database consultant. I have done some technical and commercial writing, including short articles for Transparent Language and operating manuals for QXCOM (now a part of Computer Associates). And I have taught courses on translation at the Monterey Institute of International Studies (the course is called, not surprisingly, "Translation as a Profession") and at Bellevue Community College's Translation and Interpretation Institute, and now conduct workshops for translators on a variety of subjects.

Never forget that the suite of abilities which translators possess can be applied productively to numerous related fields. Translators are often quite capable copy editors, proofreaders, and desktop publishers. Translators can readily make the transition to writing manuals for computer companies, articles for local papers or magazines, and even short stories or books. Translators can also teach the languages they know or prepare reference or educational materials. Some translators even make the move into interpretation, but be warned: interpretation is very different from translation and requires thorough schooling in the techniques of consecutive and simultaneous interpretation.

Because translation is catch-as-catch-can and can even be seasonal, having a fall-back position is a good idea, particularly as you're getting started in translation. I don't know many newcomers to the profession with a clientele that is so reliable that they have a constant and unending flow of work. You have to be ready for those dry spells. If you need money, then go get a part-time job or do something on the side. You can always work for a temporary agency. If you don't need the money, then do one of those things you talk about doing all the time.

How to Succeed

So how do people succeed in this profession? Is there a secret, and if so, what is it? And why, some people might ask, would anyone bother becoming a translator? All good questions; let's examine each in turn.

First: how to succeed. In a nutshell, you succeed by working hard. Sorry, that's really all there is to it. You can sit in your home office, watch your screen saver splash picturesque photos or swing logos around your computer monitor, and think that you are failing simply because you are an unrecognized and undiscovered genius, you are working in a language with little demand, or you don't have the right background or equipment. However, the truth is much simpler.

If you are not succeeding, you are not working hard enough. Of course, this assumes that you do have some equipment (translations hewn in stone or written on parchment are not acceptable these days), that you know a good language (little demand nowadays for Hawaiian or Basque), and that you have some ability (though if you didn't, you wouldn't be reading this book). Maybe you are the next great literary translator, the person who will bring new meaning to the Upanishads or the Iliad. But most translators are not literary geniuses, and they don't have to be.

So what do I mean? Simply this: being a freelance translator involves a lot of business and a lot of translation. You will have to spend your time marketing yourself, telling clients that you exist and are available to do work, proving to people that you can do what you say you can, and continuing to do this for the duration of your stay in the profession. No matter how long you've been a translator, you'll have to market yourself incessantly. Send your resume hither, dither, and yon. Cold call potential agencies or clients. Walk into local companies (for example: law firms and consulting houses) and see what their needs are. Contact your local Chamber of Commerce or the appropriate embassy or consulate. Get on the Web, use the directory of translation agencies at Yahoo!, go to each agency's web site, and sign yourself up as an independent contractor (also known as a translation vendor) with the agencies that let you do that online.

Unfortunately, hard work is often not enough. The industry is nowadays flooded with unskilled people all competing for the same jobs. This plus offshoring and Internet-based work exchanges has put a lot of pressure not only on rates and salaries, but also on translators themselves. There just isn't enough work to go around in many languages these days. So hard work combined with the right skills and resources, in other words a competitive language pair, strong computer skills, deep subject knowledge, and aggressive marketing, will lead to success.

Second: what's the secret? In a word: Timing. This isn't much of a secret, and saying it is much easier than doing it. Timing is everything in translation; and I mean this in the broadest sense possible. When you contact potential or existing clients, when you submit samples of your work to agencies, when you take vacations, when you make new purchases, when you pay taxes, when you get paid, and most importantly, when you submit work.

Let's start with the last first. Submitting work to an agency or client is what you have to do in order to get paid. Clients and agencies want the work on time. The top complain of project managers is late work from translators. In other words: don't submit anything late, ever! Always know and respect your deadlines. If by some chance you can't make a deadline, contact your client ahead of time to revise the delivery schedule. And keep time zones in mind: I often submit work the evening before a 9:00 a.m. delivery to a client on the East Coast.

In sum: Never submit anything late!

Next timing tidbit: set aside one third of your earnings for taxes. The government has this rule that self-employed people have to pay taxes quarterly (by April 15, June 15, September 15, and then January 15). When you do your annual income taxes, you figure out what you owe, then subtract what you've already paid and then pay the government the remainder (unless you paid too much, in which case you get some back). Pay something every quarter so that you avoid the penalties for underpayment at the end of the year and the shock of a large payment on or before April 15. If you have already paid most of what you owe at year's end, you won't have to pay much of an underpayment penalty, if anything at all.

Timing purchases: You should also plan your purchases, be they personal or business, around your finances, tax payments, and invoicing schedules. Any large business purchase is best made at the end of the year when you are close to getting your deduction for it. Any large personal expenditure is best made when you have a lot of work and a bit in money in the bank. And always keep some extra, roughly six months worth of income is a good amount to have, in the bank, just in case.

Timing vacations: Of course this depends a lot on your personal life, but it's very easy to get work around Christmas and New Year's because almost no one is around to do it. Also, during August, the supply of translators drops (they all migrate somewhere), so if you're available, it might be easier to get work. And, you should know the annual cycle for the languages you're working in so that you know when the busy and off seasons are.

Finally, timing marketing: Advertise and promote yourself regularly and consistently. Keep your profile with agencies that maintain translator databases via their website up to date. Make certain you check your listings as the busy season for your languages approaches. Also, know when to call. Project managers are very busy and don't often want to chat with translators they don't know. If you're going to call, do so midweek during the middle of the morning; this seems to be the least irritating time for project managers. When you call, be concise and constructive.

Remember, the secret is timing, and experience is the best way to master it.

Should You Be a Translator

There are many reasons to become a translator. I often hear potential translators say that they want to enter the profession because they love languages or already know two fluently. These are necessary but not at all sufficient conditions for a career in translation. You have to enjoy the task of analyzing language for meaning, then transferring that meaning from your B language into your A language. You also have to be comfortable working on tight deadlines while paying close attention to details such as terminology and formatting, using current software and hardware effectively and enthusiastically, and polishing your writing skills in your A language.

Further, you have to be very knowledgeable in a subject area that is in demand. Just knowing two languages is not enough to be a translator these days. You have to know the common concepts and facts in your subject area, along with the appropriate terminology and writing style to translate well. More and more, the subject areas that offer a lot of work are technical, mostly related to computers, biotechnology, medicine, and communications.

I translate because I like to write and I like languages. I also like my subject matter. I mostly translate original research in the fields of electrical engineering, telecommunications, and computer science. I enjoy seeing what brilliant minds in top labs around the world are working on now, often months or years before the news media or popular press pick up on it.

In general, people are in translation because they like to translate. They enjoy taking information in one language and discovering a way to render it into another. They relish the challenge of wading through uncharted linguistic and terminological waters. They feel challenged, but not frustrated, as they try to find the best way, or at least a good way, to write in their A language what the source document says in their B language. Harsh deadlines don't bother them, and, of course, they are interested in their subject matter.

Although many people enter translation by first knowing two languages and then gaining subject expertise, some become translators because they are experts in a subject area and want to combine that with a knowledge of two languages. Bilingual computer scientists, engineers, and physicians find the move into technical translation to be smooth, though not necessarily easy. Unfortunately, you won't know how you feel about translation until you actually do it. Home or classroom exercises are not the same; in school I did 2000 words of translation per week, whereas now I routinely do more than that each day, and I've been doing it every day almost 14 years. Some people find they don't like translating once they do it full-time and move on to related work.

Should You Go In-House or Freelance

In many cases the market will determine where you work, but assuming you have a choice, consider this. When you are self-employed, you are alone. You have no colleagues, co-workers, supervisor, manager, maintenance or tech-support staff. On the plus side, you can work in your pajamas while blasting acid rock; on the other hand, you have to motivate, schedule, manage, and market yourself, as well as deal with the reality of being by yourself all the time at work.

Conversely, as an employee you are surrounded by other people, often making unreasonable or unrealistic demands on your time and ability. The translator in the next cubicle may type loudly, chat on the phone often, play music on a radio, or chew gum and blow bubbles day after day. You have to do the work assigned to you when and how it is assigned, you have to deal with managers who often know only one language and consider translators to be failed writers or over-educated, over-paid bilingual secretaries.

Which is better? Ultimately your personality and working style will decide. If you can, try both. You'll quickly find out which you prefer. I am a freelance translator because I like to work for myself. I have translated in-house in Japan and have had teaching jobs on both sides of the Pacific. I've also worked as a hospital orderly, as a desktop publisher, graphic artist, database consultant, truck driver, stock boy, construction laborer, and garbage shoveler, to mention a few of my past fields of employ. At this point, I prefer working for myself, though that could change, given the right opportunity.

So is there a right reason to be a translator? I doubt it. Is there a wrong reason? Quite. Knowing two languages or loving language is not a good reason to be a translator. It's a start, of course, but there is a lot more. Loving languages is also a start, but I know people who love languages and hate translation; they seem to head into linguistics or language teaching. Knowing and loving languages, and having the skills I've described above along with the desire and discipline to work in the translation profession are the reasons to be a translator. As with many professions, you may only find out if you are really a translator by getting a job doing translation. The industry has a relatively high turnover rate, which I suspect is a result of people testing the waters and then finding them too hot or too cold. But plenty of people find them just right and stay in the field for years or even decades.

Starting Off

So you've decided this is the right career for you, and you want to be able to say that you are a translator. This is the first step in the proverbial journey of ten thousand miles. There is a well-known process, a sequence of steps people take on their way to becoming a translator, and although short cuts are possible, they are not recommended. Remember, the translation profession is not especially forgiving. It is open to all comers, and because there are so many people trying to enter, if you come unprepared, you will go unnoticed.

The translation profession in the United States currently has no universally accepted certification or accreditation required to be a translator. Nor is there a standard curriculum you must work your way through. Although the ATA does offer certification, it is only necessary for people working with Spanish and English, this due to the incredible amount of competition in that language pair. Translators working in particular fields may want or need to earn appropriate credentials or take classes, and we'll look at all of this below.

Where to Start

First, the minimum requirement to begin the process of becoming a translator is knowing two languages fluently. It does not matter how you acquire your languages. Whether you are born into a bilingual family or environment, or are educated in school, ideally starting at a young age, you must achieve adult-level fluency in your A and B languages.

Adult-level proficiency refers to a command of your languages identical to that which adults working professionally as native speakers of those languages would have. You must, in other words, be able to read, write, speak, and understand what these people would in their various professional and personal settings. In other words, high school and college-level language classes represent the initial phase of the process. You may have completed three or even four years of university coursework in Chinese or Russian or French, but that is, unfortunate to say, very little. When you can pick up a newspaper, magazine, or research article on any subject you plan to translate in, read it without using a dictionary at all, then have a discussion about its content with a professor or other person knowledgeable on the subject, and finally write a cogent "letter to the editor" about the article, you have the achieved the language facility you will need.

Okay, the above is an exaggeration. But only slightly. All of the successful translators I've known in the past two decades have that ability, or very close to it, in their languages. Achieving this will require lots of classroom and fieldwork. By classroom I mean courses that first teach you the language, and then have you function in that language doing professional-type things. By fieldwork I mean living and working in the country of your B language, ideally for years.

My own background may help clarify what I am describing. I started Japanese as a sophomore in college (better late than never), then spent my junior year in Kyoto in Japan studying at Doshisha University as an exchange student, during which time I practiced kendo with a school club, took calligraphy lessons twice a week, had four hours of Japanese language classes every day, lived with a home-stay family, and traveled extensively using youth hostels and college rail passes. Senior year back in the United States I took more Japanese classes, and after graduation I went back to Japan for two years, where I worked as an English teacher and did some basic translation work, and during which time I took advanced courses in Japanese at night, along with lots of other activities that took place in Japanese. Following that I went to graduate school for a year as a linguistics student, taking yet more classes in Japanese. I then I left my program and entered the translation school at the Monterey Institute of International Studies. In my first meeting with my advisor during orientation week I was told that my language background was wholly insufficient to be a translator and that I should go back to Japan for at least several years, perhaps even a decade, and then come back. Being a bit stubborn, I didn't do that, studied very hard at the Monterey Institute, where virtually every translation class I took was in Japanese, and finally graduated. Then I started translating. In retrospect I think my language skills could have been sharper, but more on that below.

Often overlooked are A language skills. You must become an excellent writer in your native languages, with the ability to emulate a wide variety of styles, respect the customs and conventions of your native language, and produce properly formatted, orthographically correct, well punctuated material. Take writing classes, including technical or scientific writing classes, as are available for English at many schools in the United States. Read books on the subject. My favorites for English are *The Chicago Manual of Style*, Strunk and White's *Elements of Style*, and *On Writing Well* by William Zinser. These are all classics and belong in the collection of any native English speaker who wants to translate. Also worth reading is George Orwell's *Politics and the English Language*. Further, find and read any book or article on writing for the subject area you choose to work in. Finally, read, read, read written material, particularly in your subject area, so that you are fully conversant in the style and conventions of your native language. At the Monterey Institute there was a mantra among the translation and interpretation students: a daily a day, a weekly a week, and a monthly a month. You don't have to be quite that intense, but you do need to read, read, and keep reading, along with listening, speaking, and writing, to master and maintain your language skills.

Knowledge Training

As you develop your language skills, you also need to gain a thorough grounding in one or more subject areas you can do your translation work in. A translator has to translate something, obviously, and as discussed in the first chapter, that something is a text, document, or other written material that is on a particular subject. In other words, you not only need proficiency in two languages, but also knowledge of the subject in question.

Common subject areas at present in the translation profession include scientific and technical material, in particular hardware and software documentation, medical and biotechnology materials, and telecommunications and research documents, as well as legal, financial, and sometimes more general texts, which here refers to everything from birth certificates and school transcripts to newspaper articles and website content.

The more difficult or demanding a subjects is, the greater the pay and amount of available work. If all you can do is handle simple documents like birth certificates or general news articles, you won't be able to find much work or convince an employer to hire you. If however you can translate medical instrument patents, pharmaceutical research, and bioinformatics material, you should have little difficulty finding a job.

So you will need to take at the very least university-level courses in the basics of the subject you want to work in, or through professional experience gain equivalent knowledge. If you are still in school, this should be fairly simple: take introductory physics, engineering, and calculus classes plus programming courses if you want to work on software or hardware localization, take accounting and finance courses if you want to be a financial translator, take law and policy courses if you want to be a legal translator.

Your subject knowledge will save you if your language skills flag. My Japanese, though extremely good, is not perfect, and so when I'm translating a research article on, for instance, robot vision, my knowledge of computer science and robotics helps me see what the article is talking about even if the language is obscure or abstruse. And remember, many documents will be poorly written, so again your subject knowledge will be invaluable for figuring out what the document is trying to say.

Ideally you should take courses in your subject area in both of your languages, or work professionally in your subject area using both languages. Of course this is often impractical, sometimes even impossible. So instead you can read, read, read all material you can find on your subject area in a process that is referred to as parallel reading. Texts about on the Web, including not only such multilingual sources as Wikipedia but also through industry and professional associations which maintain their Web resources in several languages. I know this seems like a lot of effort, but it is what you will have to do to become a competent professional translator.

I realize that many people, particularly in the United States, but also in other countries acquire their language skills through a liberal arts education that includes a lot of classes on literature, culture, and history, and virtually no science, mathematics, business, or other professional-type coursework. This type of background will be insufficient. Although literature is a fascinating and worthy aspect of language and is often translated, the world of literary translation is quite separate from the rest of the translation profession, and best approached by pursuing graduate-level study in your language, usually a doctorate, and then an academic career in which translating literature is a part of your profession. My undergraduate advisor was a master of modern Japanese language and literature who spent his non-teaching time translating and writing about Junichiro Tanizaki. I learned a lot from him about literary Japanese, virtually none of which has any impact on my work as a professional translator.

So learn everything you can about your languages, but stay focused on the reality of what is translated in the translation industry. Whatever your background or interests are, you should be able to find a subject area that appeals to you and is in demand for your language pair. To make certain you are heading in the right direction, find out what is in demand by looking at job listings for translators in the *ATA Chronicle*, other language publications such as *Multilingual Computing*, at translators' meetings such as the annual ATA Conference or local chapter organization gatherings, and websites including not only the obvious job search engines like Monster but also resources like Proz (www.proz.com) or Translator's Café (www.translatorscafe.com). If you don't offer what the market wants, you won't have work. So find out as early as possible how to develop your skills so that they match the realities of the market for your languages.

Experience

First of all, classroom work is experience. Regardless of how limited and artificial learning a language as an adult in a classroom is compared to acquiring one as a child in situ may be, the classroom is where most translators start. Make the most of it; go to the extra practice sessions, join the conversation club for your languages, find native speakers and spend time with them, pay a little bit for a tutor, and go to where your B language is spoken as a native language.

A classroom can only take you so far. Few if any universities offer language classes specifically for using the language in a medical, engineering, legal, or scientific context, and there are very few textbooks along such lines. So the alternative is to spend time living in the language and its attendant culture and society; this is the most efficient route to achieving the adult-level proficiency in professional, business contexts that a translator will ultimately need.

Merely traveling around a country for a few weeks or so, staying in youth hostels or hotels, hanging around bars, coffee shops, pachinko parlors (or their equivalent) will introduce you to a limited subset of the language, one that will be of little value in the translation profession. As a translator friend of mine pointed out recently, dating someone from the country of your B language will also be of limited value. After all, how many couples discuss genomics or IC design as a part of a relationship, particularly during the initial few months?

Instead, you need a job. Teaching English or another language seems to be the most common route into another country, particularly for an American with a humanities education. While not optimal, this is certainly practicable. If you take the time to read extensively, expose yourself to the language in all possible professional contexts, and challenge yourself by taking extremely advanced classes, studying for a proficiency exam, you will make ample progress in a few years.

While working you also have to continue to develop your knowledge of your eventual subject area. Again, reading is key, and coursework is useful. If you can take courses in your second language on the subject you want to work in, perfect. There is no better way to build the language foundation you will need. Often this is not possible, however, so you may have to improvise by getting textbooks, finding friends interested in the subject, and just plain pushing yourself to learn as much as possible.

I did this while in Japan by reading all of the high-school science and math textbooks used in Kawasaki City, where I was working as an English teacher, and then reading college-level textbooks in English and Japanese wherever I could find them. While in graduate school I continued this practice, advancing to reading scientific journals in Japanese, and books or articles on the science and technology. Doing this is now much easier thanks to the Web, but it was manageable in the 1980s.

Conversely, for people now living in other countries and planning a translation career with English as their second language, the situation is a bit different. Because English, American or otherwise, is so widely used and available around the world, because many countries offer such outstanding language training for their youth in English, and because some countries use English as a second language for official, diplomatic, or business purposes, the need for such people to spend one or several years in an English-speaking country like the U.S. or U.K. is limited. They can and do develop excellent language skills while growing up in their own countries. If you have such a background, take advantage of the incredible head start you've gotten; expose yourself in university or through employment to all aspects of English in the subject areas that interest you professionally. You will be that much more prepared when you start translating.

Translation Training

Finally there is the process of learning to translate. If a high level of proficiency in two languages were the necessary and sufficient requirements to be able to translate, then there should be no shortage of translators working between English and any other language in the world. Unfortunately, proficiency in two languages is merely the starting point. You also have to learn to translate.

No one at this point in time understands exactly what goes on inside translators' brains while they are translating. Such studies are probably not possible given the limited resolution of current brain scanning technology, but I await the day that we do have detailed information about this issue. Such information could easily demonstrate to an often doubtful public that translation involves more than just knowing two languages, and might help identify who can and cannot learn to translate well.

Training programs for translators have existed for upwards of four thousand years. Ancient Egypt had its School of Scribes, the Vatican has trained scholarly priests to translate since its inception, and virtually every major nation on the planet now has at least one school dedicated to training translators and interpreters.

In the United States at present, there are several types of training programs, each with at least a couple of schools. The ATA provides a booklet on the various programs available, so I'll be brief here. The Monterey Institute of International Studies and Kent State University have programs that confer an M.A. upon completion of two years of class work and a graduation project. Classes involve not only translating a lot of texts, but also studying terminology management, Machine-Assisted Translation (MAT) and other uses of computers in the translation process, and even courses on the business side of the profession. A few schools, such as the

University of Washington at Seattle and the University of Wisconsin at Madison, offer a Master's specifically for translation of a particular language pair in a scientific or technical context. The University of Hawaii and New York University (NYU), among others, offer online training programs that lead to a certificate of completion. Classes largely involve translation work. Last, Bellevue Community College and other schools around the country provide classroom certificate programs in which students start by learning about the profession and process of translation, and eventually take not only business, computer, and ethics classes, but also classes that involve actually translating.

As an aside, there are also individuals who offer workshops and seminars purporting to train translators and interpreters during a weekend or two. Such offerings tend to appear and disappear over the years, and no one in the profession believes that you can learn to translate in just a few days, so they won't be discussed in any detail here.

The majority of translators in the U.S., as stated previously, do not have formal training. However, the industry has changed a lot in the past decade. The translation profession is now listed as a hot career in books like *Cool Careers for Dummies*, and is gaining widespread recognition because of the War on Terror and some high-profile legal cases. The FBI, CIA, and other government agencies are actively and publicly recruiting translators and other language professionals. And the ATA has revamped what used to be known as the accreditation exam into what is now called the certification exam, adding among other things a continuing education requirement.

In other words, if a translator who started in the profession in the 1980s or 1990s tells you that because she didn't need any formal training you don't, think again. The question is not what did I or someone else who has been around for a long time did at the start of their careers. Though interesting, even amusing at times, and possibly inspiring, the information is rather old. You need to find out what your potential employers want you to have. If they don't care about training at all, then just make sure you can translate well. If they want some form of training, go get it.

These days, some employers, particularly the ones offering higher paying positions in technical translation or localization seem to want some form of training. Other employers don't care much at all. However, most prefer some training, if they can get it. At the same time, they will likely test your ability using a short translation test or a bilingual interview. Training, many employers know from bitter experience, does not guarantee ability, and lack of training, obviously, does not preclude it. So be prepared to demonstrate that you can translate.

When Are You Ready

How do you know when you can translate? And how do you know when you are just starting out to translate that your translations are any good? Some people believe that you just know, that they have an intuitive sense of when a translation is good, and that they felt from deep down within that they could translate. Such people represent either the gifted minority whose ability will outshine everyone else's or the misguided, even deluded majority who fall into the all-too-common trap of using language classroom standards and uninformed measures to evaluate their own work.

If you aren't sure you can translate, then you can't say where your translation may have problems. You are left with three options. First, get a job that involves a little bit of translation, one in which your work is supervised and monitored. Some firms offer internships or have junior translation positions. Other companies want, for instance, bilingual software testers or game evaluators. Such positions can offer a lot of experience, from which you can build a lot of competence and confidence.

Second, find a mentor. The ATA has a mentoring program, as do several other translation organizations. A mentor may be able to help you determine if you can translate, and what you need to do to improve your skills, but this approach has limited value. You won't really know if the mentor is a good translator, or can teach you to translate until it's too late. Further, many people in the profession believe that translation is something you can either do or you can't do, and so place little value on training. Finally, a mentor may not be able to show you how to use the software and other technologies you'll need to know, familiarize you with the subject matter you want to work on, or prepare you for a certification exam or translation test. So mentors are worth a go, but in and of themselves probably won't be enough.

Third, you can go to school. The decision to go to school to start a career represents a business decision. In business, money is always the limiting factor, by which I mean that it is the factor that more than any other determines what you should do. School costs money and time. While you are in school, you will probably make no money, so not only are you paying tuition, but you are also losing income. On the other hand, after graduation you may be able to command a higher salary, obtain a more secure position, even move faster and further on your career track.

To make this decision, you need numbers. Check the current tuition at Kent State University and the Monterey Institute, or at any other program you are interested in, then compare it with the salaries being offered by employers. Further, contact the program director to find out what the graduates are doing and what their income is. You want to know not only what the graduates from last year are up to, but also what those from five and ten years ago are doing now. Then talk to a couple of current students and recent graduates to see how they feel about their investment. Last, talk to several potential employers or look at job postings to find out if education is preferred or rewarded in any substantial way.

Your path into the translation profession can follow one of several routes. No one at this point can say which is better. I know people with graduate-level educations in translation and people with no formal training whatsoever. I also know that the demands in the profession vary depending on the language and subject you are working one. This is, as described above, why I cannot be more specific. Of course, what we're trying to do here is determine beforehand, possibly years beforehand, whether or not an employer will reward you with a job, maybe even at a higher salary, after you complete a training program. As Niels Bohr said, "prediction is difficult, especially about the future."

Career Paths

You are ready to take your first position as a translator with a company, or your first job as a freelancer. You feel great, all your hard work, study, practice, and in some cases preparation for and passing exams has paid off. You are ready to translate, and to be paid for it.

But there is more. Translation as a profession implies that translation is a career, or it can be if you approach it in the right way. Because translation is generally viewed as a craft or skill, much as accounting or computer programming is, the possible career paths are varied, and depend on your personality and skill set, professional preferences, and what happens next in the industry.

So let's first look at some general trends. According to Jeff Wood, Director of Career and Enrollment Management at the Graduate School of Translation and Interpretation at the Monterey Institute of International Studies, there are several important forces at play in the industry.

First, there is downward pressure on rates for freelance translators and income for in-house translators. As he put it when asked: "Don't go into T&I (translation and interpretation) to make money." Income potential was already discussed earlier, so you know the limits. Translation is like nursing or accounting: a good middle-class living, with a few exceptional and talented individuals with high levels of training making far above the average. This pressure is coming from competition from overseas and increased use of technology, which is discussed at length in the chapter called MT & MAT.

Second, Jeff Wood expects more and more employers to require credentials of some form from potential translators, freelance or in-house. This trend is consistent with what is happening in many other industries: sheepskins are becoming more important as a way to verify a person's ability. Also, companies are facing fierce competition and no longer want to train new hires as much as they used to.

Third, more and more employers are becoming picky about technical skills, requiring translators to be comfortable with a wide variety of computer-related technologies, from Machine-Assisted Translation software to programming languages and tools, particularly for the Web and computer games.

Fourth, for in-house translators, the key question is: "can you do more than one thing?" A translator who can only translate is not much of an asset as compared to one who can build and maintain terminology or translation memory databases, or can work on the company's website. In other words, in-house translators and interpreters are more likely to find and keep good jobs if they can also perform administrative work, handle project management tasks, work with translation memories or terminology databases, and even do some sales work, negotiating and planning projects with clients.

Finally, Jeff Wood expects there to be fewer in-house positions available in the coming years. First, a clarification: Jeff divides the in-house world into three major groups. First are the large corporations. They pay the highest (salaries in the $40s on average), and often are not American companies but foreign companies with a large presence or operation in the United States (think Honda, Toyota, Siemans). You may have to work outside the U.S., where there are more in-house opportunities than there are here to get a job with one of these large companies. Second are the large translation companies, Lionbridge for instance, which pay almost as well as the large corporations, but ask a lot of their translators and interpreters, and often work people very hard. Finally, there are small agencies, "mom-and-pop" operations that sit neatly in a niche market. Although the pay isn't as high, the opportunities to learn, acquire new skills, and do a wider variety of tasks abound, and work in such firms can serve as a springboard to a job with a large corporation or translation company.

All that said, opportunities still abound, in particular for high-demand languages and subject areas. You can easily brush up your knowledge of a new subject area, or if you want to work in-house, learn one or more of the skills mentioned above. So there is no need to panic. Trends are what they are: what you have to do is adapt.

First Steps

Translators translate, so if you are a translator, you are going to translate. For however long you are in the translation profession, you are going to translate. There are, however, a variety of other tasks in the translation process that translators can and do become involved in.

First, however, you have to get started. As hinted at briefly in the first three chapters, not all languages and subject areas are equal in the translation industry at present. Your fate in the translation profession, particularly at the beginning, will depend in no small part on factors you have no control over. This may be unfortunate and painful to realize, but it is what happens.

I've seen many fine, talented translators complete training programs or even degrees only to discover that their skills are not in demand in the translation marketplace because their language combination is too obscure or too well populated by competent, established people, their subject expertise is too limited for them to do anything but the most elementary work, or their skills with the software tools necessary for translators are insufficient.

Languages like Spanish and French are too commonly known in the United States for a newcomer to have an easy time getting work. Further, such languages don't pay well because of the law of supply and demand, which in terms of the translation profession states that if there is a given demand for translation in one language and the supply of translators rises, then the rates paid to the translators will fall. Conversely, languages like Japanese and Chinese are sufficiently rare and the demand for translation sufficiently high that if you have the requisite skills, you will do better in general than someone with Spanish or French.

I know this will disappoint those of you who have spent years mastering the language of Cervantes or Voltaire, but I would rather share this now than have you unprepared. By the time you are ready to consider being a translator you have already invested heavily in your languages. Although it is always possible to learn another one, you know well what it took to learn those you already know.

If you have one of these language pairs, consider instead developing secondary skills if you want to work in-house or offering ancillary services if you want to be an independent contractor. Translation agencies and those companies that hire translators full-time will be more inclined to hire you if you have strong computer skills, including with MAT software like Trados, if you have desktop publishing or graphic arts skills, or if you have editing skills. Freelance translators when first starting can gain experience and income by teaching or tutoring people in their languages, getting involved in home-based telephone interpreting, and even just temping through agencies like Parker, Kelly, or

Manpower, all of which, by the way, I did during my first year as a freelance translator.

Also, don't overlook other skills you have. I've heard of would-be Spanish/English translators who somehow forget they have a CPA (Certified Public Accountant). The combination of language skills and accounting can sell well. Further, some people start out doing both translation and interpretation, as have a number of colleagues of mine, and then the market determines whether they focus on translation, interpretation, or continue doing both.

The First Job

Where and how you start in the translation profession will depend on the languages you know, what if any training or certification you have, and what subject are you can handle. As stated above, some language pairs will prove very difficult to find good work in, while others will be easier. So don't take personally a failure to find work; you may have to consider less apparent options or even a different career path altogether.

A search on major job sites on the Web using "translation," "localization," "bilingual," or the name of a particular language as keywords inevitably yields positions in localization, positions involving translation, project management positions in a translation agency or company that is active in several countries, software, hardware, and games testing, law enforcement and military positions, to mention just a few. Many of these positions are for work going from English into other languages, usually not the languages Americans study in high school or college.

The following statistics make this point nicely. According to the Education Life section (p. 21) of the *New York Times* (Nov. 11, 2001), in 1998 the eight percent of college students were studying foreign languages were mostly taking Spanish, French, or German (90%). This means that less than one percent of American college students were studying other languages. Also worth keeping in mind: few college students ever go beyond the second-year level.

In other words, although few Americans ever become highly proficient in a second language, the majority of the translation positions require a native language other than English. When the position requires English as a native language, the second language is often one of those "one percenters," a language like Japanese,

Chinese, Korean, or Arabic. So competition may make your entry into the profession difficult.

What to do? There are many possibilities. First, you may be able to find a translation position for your language pair and in your subject area. However, because many employers prefer experience translators, you may have to start with a different type of work. Such work includes bilingual testing of computer hardware, software, or games, staff positions in companies in which translation is a part of your duties, or if you are attempting to become a full-time freelance translator, jobs that involve editing, proofreading, desktop publishing, or related work for translation agencies instead of translating itself.

Since many translators learn their trade on the job, an obvious question emerges: how do they get such a job without already having experience? The answer is that for entry-level positions, particularly outside of the United States, translation may be one of a variety of language-related tasks such people are hired for. For instance, I did my first translation work for the City of Kawasaki Board of Education when I was on the JET Program in Japan in 1987. Although hired as an Assistant English Teacher, my Japanese language skills resulted in occasional requests for translation from Japanese into English. In a similar fashion, many translators cut their teeth in the profession.

So the basic strategy for getting your first job is this: take whatever you can get wherever you can get it and push it for all it's worth. Getting that first job will be easier if you have a degree or certification in translation, and you may be able to go straight from school into a full-time position with a company, or get set up as a freelance translator in relatively short order.

But to get that first job you have to be flexible and creative. This may include being willing to move to a different country. Americans with Spanish, French, or German as their second language find getting their first job as a translator much easier if they relocate to Europe, or in the case of Spanish, Latin America as well. The U.N. has a massive operation in Switzerland, as does the World Trade Organization and the World Intellectual Property Organization. Ireland is a hotbed of localization activity, and London offers numerous opportunities for business, financial, and legal translation.

Although I started in 1993, meaning that my experiences are a bit out of date, I began marketing myself to translation agencies and companies, hundreds of them, months before my graduation in May.

I then continued this, while also teaching Japanese and English at a small, private language school in town, working as a telephone interpreter for AT&T Language Line, and offering up my computer skills to all local companies. It took about six months before my income from translation alone covered all my expenses. So at that point I started phasing out the other, less lucrative or enjoyable activities, and focused on building my translation business. I continued aggressive marketing, sending out hundreds of resumes every few months, and contacting agencies in person or by phone. It was a demanding period, at times grueling, but paid off with more work from better clients with each passing year.

Your path will be different. But if you have the skills to translate and a few other related skills to offer, the drive to find potential employers, the willingness to relocate or take short-term jobs, and the patience to see through the first few months or even years before you are well-established, respected, and recognized, you will make it.

Foreseeable Forces and Factors

The dominant factor in the translation profession since the mid-1990s has been the Internet. The high-tech boom of the late 1990s created rapid growth in the localization industry, which became the tail that wagged the translation dog for several years. Although the dot-com boom is long over, the Internet continues to influence how and where translators do business.

The advent of online job sites such as Proz.com and Translator's Café (translatorscafe.com) have introduced a new model for doing business in the translation profession. Translation agencies and businesses that need to have translations done can offer work directly to freelancers, who bid against each other to win the job. This is created considerable downward pressure on prices in the translation market, particularly for language pairs available in two or more countries in which the cost of living and the cost of doing business differ considerably.

Although such sites represent an interesting opportunity for new translators as well as a good way for freelance translators to find work, like auction sites there is little accountability for individuals or organizations that cheat, and little quality control, particularly in regards to the ability of an individual translator to do good work or the capacity of an organization to pay in a timely fashion for the work.

Nevertheless, such sites will continue to flourish and represent one common path by which translation work is done. When quality, reliability, or secrecy are paramount for a project, translation agencies still prefer to work directly with someone they know, and so such sites do not now and will not in the foreseeable future take over the industry.

The other critical factor influencing the translation profession is Machine Assisted Translation (MAT) and Machine Translation (MT) software. MAT provides a variety of forms of assistance to a translator, particularly when working on a large project, or a project that is similar to one the translator has done previously. MT ideally provides finished copy in the target language, though the reality at present varies from acceptable quality for certain purposes to garbled text we call word salad.

More and more translators are required to use MAT software, and few find themselves in a position to do all of their work without it. As long as you have an electronic version of the source document, translation memory containing terminology or useful concurrences, and material that is redundant or repetitive, the software improves productivity, particularly in terms of accuracy and consistency with terminology and phraseology. The cost of such products, particularly Trados, remains prohibitive for many freelance translators, however. Further, Trados in particular is losing ground to other software packages because of its high cost and large number of bugs.

In translation agencies and companies, these products are so commonly used that job applicants must already be comfortable with them. Many freelance jobs, as can be seen by viewing the listings in Translators' Café or Proz, also require such technologies. The translator who does not take the time to become well-versed with them will ultimately be without work.

Career Paths

Once you have started in the translation profession, there are several possible career paths. The first and most common is to continue translating, often working at a higher level with more challenging material and at a higher salary. Eventually you may become a senior translator, the person in charge of a group of translators all working in the same languages or even in charge of all of the translators in an organization. People in such positions spend part of their time translating, and the rest of their time training and evaluating their staff, managing the ongoing projects, and dealing with the technology the group uses.

In larger companies the senior translator is distinct from a translation manager. While the senior translator will be the most experienced and competent member of the team, whose responsibilities may include hiring and training, working on translation technologies like MAT tools, and preparing terminology databases, the translation manager may be an individual with little if any translation or language skills but with the requisite business and management ability. On the other hand, often translators can become translation managers, particularly in organizations that want such managers to have a clear, complete understanding of translators and the work they do.

A project manager is an individual in a translation company or in the translation division of an organization who oversees the translation projects, assigning specific sections of material to individual translators, keeping track of productivity and progress in various jobs, evaluating technologies for use in the translation process, working with clients and vendors to prepare quotes for a translation project or deliver a completed job, and handling any and every problem that arises with the staff, outside vendors, or the technology. Such people must be able to multitask to an incredible degree, be cool and confident under pressure, and be willing to work often long hours. Although a background in translation or language is not required for such positions, it is obviously extremely helpful, and so not surprisingly this is a frequent preference, particularly in translation agencies.

A localization manager is similar to a project manager in terms of job duties and personality. The difference is that a localization manager works for a single firm, usually a high-tech firm, and is focused on the preparation of corporate materials in foreign languages. There are many levels of localization managers, with responsibility and the size and scope of projects increasing as one rises to higher levels. Knowledge of common localization tools and technologies (including, for instance, Trados, Catalyst, or Deja-Vu), as well as standard documentation management and project management tools (including, for instance, Microsoft Project, XML, and website management software) is vital for such positions.

Another possibility is terminologist. Large-scale translation operations, particularly localization operations or any other situation in which MAT software is used regularly, require precise, ongoing management of the terminology used in the translations. This task usually falls to a full-time terminologist, an individual with a strong background in translation or linguistics and with the requisite subject knowledge to define precisely and accurately in two or more languages the terminology to be used in the translations. The terminologist typically works closely with both translators and translation managers, and must have a good command of common software tools for translation, along with database software.

There are, of course, other positions and other opportunities to use one's translation skills, but they are sufficiently obscure and unusual that they will not be discussed here. Often, creativity and resourcefulness are invaluable when looking for a new, more challenging and lucrative position within the translation profession.

Making the Most of It

Long-term success in the translation profession requires not only dedication to your languages, but also a willingness to continually improve your knowledge of translation technologies and maintain your expertise in the subject areas you work it. The ATA now requires continuing education credits to maintain certification, as is common in many other professions.

Successful translators will have to routinely attend classes, workshops, and seminars in order to stay on top of their profession and abreast of all new developments. Fortunately, the annual ATA conference, specialty conferences given around the year by the ATA and other organizations, classes and workshops held at local community colleges, and seminars given by chapter organizations of the ATA all represent good opportunities for translators to continue their education.

There is, however, a tendency for translators not to stay the profession for very long. Rare is the translator has 10 or more years of full-time, continuous experience in the field. Many move on to related professions, change careers entirely, or simply stop working to devote time to raising a family (this, of course, is more common for women). The reasons translators leave the profession vary considerably, though naturally income and job satisfaction are the primary motivations.

There also seems to be a certain degree of burnout, particularly among translators who have to work very hard at low rates in order to earn enough to scrape by during the first couple of years in the freelance market. The amount of work coupled with the low income and little prospect for improvement has led to a number of disgruntled translators who have left the industry for greener pastures. Finally, some translators succumb to repetitive strain injuries (RSI) such as carpal tunnel syndrome or thoracic outlet syndrome. Although technologies such as voice input software can compensate, many people find it easier to change careers.

There does not seem to be an "old translators' home." I personally know several translators who retired in their 60s after a long and successful career, and I know translators who left the profession after 2, 5, or even 10 years of work. Ultimately, how your career evolves will depend on a variety of factors that you cannot anticipate until they happen. The important thing is to make the most of your career while you are working in the translation profession, and if the time to leave does come, then to do so gracefully and move onto something else.

Translation Agencies

Translation works ultimately comes from some individual or organization that has material in one language and needs to have it in another language. As discussed in the first two chapters, most of this material is business-related, often it is software or hardware manuals, engineering specifications, financial reports, or legal transcripts; in other words, material that someone needs for some business purpose. Frequently the material is too large and complex for one translator to handle in the time allotted, and typically the organization that wants the translation prefers to give the entire translation project to one firm. So we have translation vendors, typically referred to as translation agencies or companies.

A translation agency is not the same as a translation company. An agency is of course a company, insofar as it is legally incorporated, but it functions as a go-between that provides services including project management, desktop publishing, printing, re-programming websites or software, while having freelance translators handle the actual translation. Although some agencies do have a few translators on staff to handle jobs that come in on a regular basis, such translators also have to have other skills, as discussed in the previous chapter, to work successfully in an agency.

Translation agencies tend to specialize, filling niches in the industry wherever possible. Some agencies work only with one or a group of related languages, while others specialize in a certain subject area. There are agencies that handle only Japanese or Spanish, and there are those that deal exclusively with legal translation. All of these niches represent small markets, but they are large enough to create thousands of jobs and ample opportunity for freelance translators.

A translation company, by contrast, is a larger organization, that handles the entirety of a translation project using its own internal resources for the most part. Lionbridge is the best known, and largest, translation company as of 2006, and has offices around the world, handling translation projects for companies like Microsoft, Boeing, and others. A translation company can easily take on a project involving twenty or thirty languages, for instance producing the localized editions of the new version of the Windows operating system, or the documentation necessary to performance maintenance and repair on a 747. A translation agency is not large enough nor has the resources to work on projects of that size.

Many translators work in a translation company or agency. Freelance translators frequently work with agencies, and occasionally even work with translation companies. Of course, many translators work for government agencies or in the military, or for a company that has a translation department to handle its translation needs.

In this chapter we will look closely at translation agencies in particular, since they are the largest source of work for freelance translators and a good source of employment for in-house translators. But the focus here will be for freelance translators looking for clients.

Why Translators Need Agencies

Freelance translators have all had to deal with agencies at some point or another. Although some work exclusively with agencies, and others have their own clients, most work with a mixture of the two. In-house translators sometimes work for a company or organization, but more often than not are found in translation companies, agencies, or other organizations that need translators. No translator can afford to ignore translation agencies, and it behooves every translator to know as much about them s possible.

Always remember that translation agencies are first and foremost businesses. Like all other forms of business, they live and die by their ability to turn a profit. And their ability to turn a profit rests firmly in their capacity to find good translators and work successfully with them. In other words, translators are the lifeblood of an agency. A translation agency without translators will go out of business immediately. An agency must have translators and prefers to have good, reliable translators. The opposite, however, is not necessarily true. Many translators work with end-clients directly, providing most of the services that agencies do. Most translators, however, myself included, get at least some of their work from agencies.

So if a translation agency does nothing more than provide translation services, why do translators need them? Why can't translators simply work for the end-client directly, cut out the middle, and make lots more money? Why in this age of Internet-based commerce, corporate streamlining, and outsourcing cannot an individual translator work directly with, for instance, Microsoft? There are three reasons.

First, the size of translation projects. Many translation jobs consist of hundreds or thousands of pages of material, perhaps one or more manuals, technical documentation, or legal materials. The end-client, the one that contracts with the agency to do the translation work, wants the job completed too quickly for a single translator to ever do, such as two weeks for 250,000 words of material, and prepared professionally, perhaps printed in full color with graphics and photos. In other words, no single translator has the capacity to provide this scale of service for projects of this size.

Second, the nature of translation projects. Often a translation job will involve translating material into five languages at once, such as with the preparation of an annual report or the manuals for a new software package. Again, the end-client wants it all returned quickly, so no single translator, even assuming that one translator has the ability to translate into five different languages, a virtual impossibility, can hope to finish the job.

Third, the nature of end-clients. End-clients usually prefer to deal with the same organization on a regular basis. This simplifies their business operations considerably. What this means is that an individual translator cannot reasonably hope to provide all the different services, including various languages, subject areas, desktop publishing, offset printing, and so forth, that an end-client might need during a given business year. Once again, the demands of many end-clients are far beyond what a single translator can provide.

A case in point for translation agencies: When a computer game developer in France wants to bring its game to the international market, it may need to have the game rewritten in places to accommodate the new languages, and it will want to have the game ready to go on the market as quickly as possible. There are agencies that specialize in computer games, since it is a large, lucrative market. Some translation companies might also deal with computer games, but typically the size of the project is too small to interest them.

So what does a translation company do? For instance, when Microsoft prepares to release a new version of its operating system, it wants to ship the completed software to every market at the same time, what is known in the software business as "sim-ship." This means that the software and all its documentation has to be translated from English into over a dozen languages all at once in a matter of months. Clearly a large translation company will be involved, since no translation agency, to say nothing of an individual translator, could even handle the workload for one language pair, let alone all of the languages, as well as the screen shots, graphics, and other elements of a finished product and everything else that has to be ready on the ship date.

Agencies therefore play a crucial role in the translation industry, and because they rely on freelance translators to handle the translation work, they are an invaluable source of jobs. Furthermore, because of the Internet, a freelance translator can potentially work with translation agencies anywhere in the world, and vice-versa. Location does not matter.

What Agencies Do

So there are the translation agencies. They provide two categories of service. One: they put together the number of translators needed to handle the material in question, and some agencies maintain an in-house translation staff to handle languages with high, steady demand. Two: they manage the project from start to completion, including project estimates and bids, desktop publishing, layout, and typesetting, localization of content (both text and visual material), graphics, and printing. Translators therefore are a one of many essential parts of the overall translation process.

Agencies, at least good ones, also simplify a translator's life. The agency calls, tells you there is work to be done, you briefly discuss the job with someone you know and trust, then you do the work, submit it along with an invoice, and you get paid. You don't have to deal with submitting invoices to a huge corporation, a task which can be something of a nuisance, explaining to people with no knowledge of language and translation why your translation doesn't look exactly like the original, telling people with no experience living in other cultures why a particular friendly hand gesture in the United States is lewd in Brazil or meaningless in Taiwan. Most important, you don't have to deal with as much marketing, something the agencies do as a matter of course.

Agencies benefit from having good translators available because they can then provide their clients with quality products in a timely fashion. Agencies definitely want to have good translators, are willing to pay good translators more, and will often be very flexible with you when they want you in particular to do a job for them. Note the reciprocal relationship here. Not only do translators need agencies to get work, but agencies need translators to get their work done. Agencies need translators as much as translators need agencies because each group provides skills and services the other requires to survive. For biology buffs, this is symbiosis at its best. Agencies are not parasites, sucking profit away from translators. Nor are translators like remora or pilot fish, tagging along with the agency shark to snap up leftover tidbits. A freelance translator who refuses to consider working with agencies, looking down upon those who do, is naive at best, and probably doomed to fewer business opportunities in the long run.

Translators do from time to time band together to provide the services that an agency provides in an attempt to circumvent what some translators see as a source of lost income. However, they typically find that this requires a considerable investment in computer hardware, software, and training, not to mention finding reliable printing service bureaus and such. All of this is specialized work, outside the skill set most translators have developed. Color separations, image manipulation, layout, typesetting, and so forth require knowledge and experience. Some groups of translators do cultivate these skills or hire people who have them, but by the time they do all of this and create a successful, functional group, they have in essence become a translation agency.

Now what about those projects that don't require fancy printing, DTP, or color separations? In practice, agencies tend to handle those because they come from the same people who have the larger projects. End-clients like simplicity, so they work consistently with the same agency.

However, many translators do develop their own clients and translate such "simpler material" for them. About half my work comes from agencies and half comes from direct clients. It is a good situation because the agencies I work with are responsible and competent and pay me fairly, and my direct clients are the same. Reaching this position requires time and effort, however, as well as no small amount of luck.

Nevertheless, most translators work for agencies at some point in their careers. Even if you want to work exclusively with direct clients, the marketing procedure remains very similar. In other words, there is a lot of business to take care of before you will be inundated with translation work.

Contacting Agencies

The first thing you have to do is tell agencies that you exist. You should do this in as many different ways as possible, including registering as a freelance translator (also called translation vendor) on the websites of agencies that offer this feature, and most do these days, joining the ATA or local translator associations and having yourself listed in their directories, or attending conferences and symposiums for translators where you might hand out business cards or other material.

Most agencies do have a Web-based registration service for freelance translators. You can find their URLs through, for instance, the Yahoo! business section, which lists many of the translation agencies currently operating in the United States. Other lists can be found through the ATA, common business directories, and even the Yellow Pages, available for the whole country in most libraries as well as through Web searches.

Note that the days of mailing printed resumes to prospective translation agencies are over. Although many organizations do still expect and appreciate being contacted by mail, the translation industry has evolved to the point that, as one project manager told me recently, a resume received by mail is summarily dismissed.

Most Web-based registration systems for freelance translators still require a resume, submitted in electronic format. Though MS Word is the most common format, some organizations shun this, so have two versions of your resume available: one in MS Word and the other in plain text format.

Your Resume

Your resume has to be distinctive and meaningful. It is a proof of concept, a demonstration in brief that you are a capable, reliable translator worth the risk of working with. Project managers at agencies receive 50 or even 100 resumes per week. Given their myriad responsibilities, they give each resume less than 10 seconds of attention. So your resume has to stand out, to cry out that you are *the* translator for this agency, that you are the one worth contacting and working with. How exactly you do this is more than a little difficult to say, but I suggest you consult many different books on resume writing to look at samples, then find a format and style which appeals to you, next spend a lot of time working your information into that format, and finally put in the effort to check the results, preferably by having a friend (or ideally, a friend who is a project manager) critique your efforts.

There are certain fundamental elements for a translator's resume. It must include the following information:

- Your full name (the one you want on paychecks)
- Your business address (which is probably your home address as well)
- Your telephone and fax number(s)
- Your email address

All of this information must appear at the very top of the resume, where it can be seen immediately.

Next, and so important that if you omit it some agencies will stop reading your resume, comes your native and working languages. Don't claim to have more than one native language. I know some agencies which throw away resumes of translators who claim to have two or three native languages. Also, be very careful about claiming to translate into your non-native languages. Some agencies will instantly recycle your resume if they read something to that effect.

Of course there are individuals who by birth or training have achieved native fluency in more than one language, as there are people who can translate into their second languages. Such people are quite rare, however, and so claiming to be one of them is risky if only because agencies have been burned enough times to be wary. You are better off claiming less at first and then doing more later for a client than the other way around.

After this material, list in detail your experience as a translator, including work you've done in any country, for any organization, under any circumstances. If your background is so extensive that it would fill volumes, then pick the best and omit the rest. Also, make sure to list currently active clients, as well as those you've worked for in the past. Specify the work you did for them. Don't just say: I translated for ABC Corp. Say: Translated user's manual for Blah-blah software for ABC Corp. in 2005.

Describe your educational background, highlighting all aspects related to translation, language, or the area you translate in. If you have a Bachelor's in languages or literature, put it in. If you plan to translate engineering material and hold a B.S. in engineering, put it in. If you have unrelated degrees, put them in, but do not emphasize them. If you have absolutely no educational background in language, translation, or the subject you want to work on, you should get some.

If you are just starting out as a translator and have no translation experience, put your education first on your resume, consider emphasizing those aspects of your academic training which demonstrate your language and translation ability. One way or another you need to convince the agency or organization that you can actually translate. Nothing speaks more clearly than experience, and specialized education is a form of experience.

Next describe any other related experience which will help demonstrate that you can translate and that you know your languages. Specify how long you have spent abroad, how much language training you've had for your non-native languages, and how much education and experience you've had in the fields you translate in. Do not mention menial jobs in college, part-time summer work, or other unrelated professional experience. You do not want to bore people. Most importantly, nothing from before college should be on your resume.

Finally, make sure to mention any awards, certifications, accreditation, professional memberships and other qualifications or accomplishments related to your languages or translation. If you received a scholarship for one of your languages, mention it. If you passed the ATA exam or a high-level language proficiency test, put it on your resume.

At this point your resume may already be looking full, so eliminate anything that isn't completely relevant. A resume is a "best of" list, a selection of highlights, not a complete personal history. Although a two-page resume may be tolerated, you are far better off having a one-page version ready, since it is what you will usually use.

For reference I have created some sample resumes and put them on the Language Realm, this book's companion website. Use these samples to get ideas for your resume, not necessarily as a format or style that is absolutely required in the industry. Remember, it's the content not the style of your resume that will get you jobs. Style without substance is at best entertaining for a few seconds. Substance will take you far even if it lacks style.

Cover Letters

You won't need a cover letter when registering yourself with a Web-based system run by a translation agency. There are, however, agencies that prefer potential translators to submit a resume to their "vendor relations" staff, which means you'll need a cover letter. Also, if you are contacting a potential direct client or applying for a full-time position, a cover letter is essential.

First and foremost, the cover letter should state what kind of work you do and want. Don't just say: I am a translator; say: I am a freelance translator of Japanese and English working in the biomedical and computer fields. Then you should go on to say that you are looking for work as an independent contractor or full-time employee. Finally, use the cover letter to emphasize whatever experience and qualifications you have that would qualify you as a translator.

The cover letter should be succinct, simple, and elegant. It should not extend to a second page, nor contain a single typographical, grammatical, or other error of language form or function. You may generate cover letters from a PIM or other business software, but the letter should still retain personal touches, such as a handwritten signature, unless it is being submitted electronically via email. You should also include a contact name when possible. If not, a simple greeting like "Hello" is sufficient, if not particularly elegant.

In the cover letter you want to mention how long you have been a freelance translator, when you are available if you are not available at all times, and what kind of work you handle. Do not mention rates, except in general. You want to be flexible and marketable. Cover letters have a way of being ignored for weeks or even months, and sometimes are stored for years in translation agencies. If two years ago you sent a letter quoting a rate, you might not want to be asked to work at that rate now. Moreover, since every job is different, you want room to maneuver in your negotiations.

The Waiting Game

Anyone who has worked as a freelance translator realizes that there is no way to tell who is a translator and who isn't. Any idiot can claim to be a translator. Some, it would seem, do. The only obvious limitation is that you have to know at least two languages. So agencies have to sift through all the resumes they receive and figure out who is a bona fide translator capable of accurately rendering information from one language into another. They have to determine who is up to the job. Because there is no universally accepted system for training or accrediting translators, at least not at present in the United States, agencies and direct clients are left with two basic methods: look at the person's background or give a test.

Many agencies are unlikely to accept at face value accreditation or claims of former translation experience. Remember, there is virtually no way for them to corroborate your claims of having been a translator in Ulan Bator. Further, credential fraud is on the rise. Unless you have a degree or certificate from a well-known translation program, your claims will be questioned. So the other alternative is to use translation tests. Also, having degrees and accreditations does not necessarily exempt you from testing, as I well know from experience.

To this day I am taking translation tests. Colleagues of mine who have been in the profession as long as I have are also taking translation tests for jobs with new employers or to start a working relationship with a new client. There are two things about these tests you need to be aware of. First, they are evaluated using unknown standards by people who may or may not be capable of making a sound judgment about your performance. So don't be surprised if you fail a test that you feel confident about. I have several times. It happens. Second, the tests are often long enough to absorb several hours or more of your time, so set aside a period when you won't be interrupted. I often end up taking these tests on weekends, when I'd otherwise not be doing anything related to my business. Getting the test done properly and returning it on time is all you can do. After that, it's watch and wait and see.

If you are asked to do a test, complete it promptly. The first virtue in the translation profession is punctuality, and your first opportunity to demonstrate this to a potential client is by responding in a timely fashion to any request they make. Remember, the agencies have the money and need to get their translation work done.

So they can make certain demands of translators. It behooves translators to cooperate cheerfully with this process, not because it is pleasant, but because the translation industry is a meritocracy: if you can do the work, you will have work.

Some agencies or direct clients will accept a sample translation from you in lieu of a test. Others, however, will show no interest in sample material you send them. In fact, submitting samples before they are asked for is a waste of effort. Most agencies trust their own tests over a sample you send. Should you be asked to submit a sample, make sure you have the legal right to submit the material. Remember that as an independent contractor who works on a for-hire basis, you do not own the rights to what you translate.

So here you are, ready, willing, and able to translate, and patiently waiting for the agencies or direct clients you have contacted to give you work. Translation vendors however do not want to be the first organization to give you work; they prefer to have translations handled by experienced people. This leads to an inevitable paradox: how do you get your first translation job.

The answer is time and patience. Even with degrees and accreditation, you are still an unknown to a translation agency or direct client. Even if the agency gives you a sample translation test and you pass, you are still an unknown. So you have to wait for the opportunity to prove yourself to arise. This comes when for whatever reason the agency needs a translator and you make it to the top of the list.

Typically an agency or direct client has a stable of freelance translators they call upon when translation work needs to be done. Project managers even have favorite translators, and if you are not already in this group, you have to wait. Your turn comes when the agency can't find anyone else to do a translation. I've seen this happen because the regular translator was away on vacation, had retired, took a break to give birth to a child, or was injured in an automobile collision, to name a few possibilities. In other words, harsh though this may seem, your turn will come, if only because change and disaster are an inevitable part of life. Your turn may also come when an agency or direct client grows, takes on new projects, or expands into new areas of business. But even when your big break does come, it will in all likelihood not be particularly large. Instead, agencies tend to start new translators off with small assignments, so as to test their ability and cultivate a friendly, trusting relationship. In time, and often the time is brief, you will have as much work from a client as the client is in a position to give.

Responses

After you send out your cries for work, you might have to wait a few weeks or even months before the replies come, assuming they come at all. Many agencies, not to mention potential direct clients, will not respond at all unless and until they have a particular need for you. Some sort through all resumes received or online registrations once per month, or even once a quarter, and then send responses to those queries that both impress them and are relevant to what they do. In other words, be patient. No news is not necessarily good news or bad news.

The replies that do come will not necessary be offers of work, either. Many agencies automatically respond to a resume or website registration by sending a thank-you letter, usually via email, and one or more forms for you to fill out. Fill these out and send them back fast. I know of one agency that uses those forms as a kind of test; if you can't get it back to them within 15 days, they aren't interested anymore. Some agencies even tell you to get it back to them fast. So spend the time it takes to deal with this material when it comes; doing so is a part of business, and if you are self-employed, the responsibility is yours.

The forms that many agencies send will seem redundant. You'll have to fill in your name, address, educational and professional background, and equipment. You'll also have to detail your rates (more on that in a bit), your daily, weekly, monthly, and yearly (or at least one of these) output, and other information. If you're not sure about something on these forms, call the agency. This is a great way to get to talk to someone there, develop a closer relationship, and even tell them some of the more intangible things about yourself.

Agencies may also send an independent contractor form, a standard legal document that says that you are working independently on a work-for-hire basis. Your translations belong to the agency, not to you. You, however, are liable for any errors, omissions, delays, or other problems which occur in the process of translating something. Read this form carefully: some agencies make peculiar demands in these forms. For instance: translators must carry $500,000 in liability insurance; translators must redo all work until it satisfies the client; or, translators are expected to comply with all demands of the agency and client.

These demands can be trying, particularly the one about insurance. I have consulted several attorneys and employment specialists and found that such errors and omissions insurance is not necessary. Translators are poor candidates for lawsuits and the insurance itself is very expensive for the coverage offered. Remember that companies sue not so much on principle as to recover damages, real or perceived. Translators are poor by corporate standards, and so are unlikely to become a target for a lawsuit. Further, the coverage itself, whether it is errors and omissions insurance or some other form of professional liability coverage, may not do what you want. More fundamentally, however, is the fact that translators are one step in a lengthy process (step four out of ten, in the view of one project manager I know), and so blaming the translator exclusively is legally irresponsible. Translators, ideally at least, work on a "good-faith, best-effort" policy, informing clients of all problems and issues in their translations, and discussing the future of the document. Of course, you should consult with an attorney or other professional to confirm the situation in your locale, and to make certain there is nothing about your situation that justifies insurance.

You may be tempted to contact potential clients by telephone, whether or not you have already sent a resume or filled in a Web-based form. Doing so can be a great way to make a brief personal introduction, but always be succinct and gentle. Ask if the person you want to talk to has time. If the person says yes, then give a brief, focused description of yourself. Do not attempt to talk up a project manager; they are generally far too busy to engage in chit-chat with a translator they don't know or work with. Also, calling on Tuesdays, Wednesdays, or Thursdays seems preferable, insofar as the work week is neither just starting nor ending. Finally, save the calls for potential clients that you really want to work for. Such phone calls are similar to job interviews: challenging and at times stressful. In other words, they take effort. So put your effort where it will most likely yield useful results.

Getting started as a freelance translator can be a time-consuming, trying experience. Some people will find a steady supply of work quickly while others will simply never have enough to live on. Although your language combination and subject expertise will greatly influence their entry into the world are freelance translation, at the same time fate, fortune, or circumstance (whatever you want to call it) will play a substantial role. If you find yourself without work as a freelancer, consider employment in-house, or consider the other ways to use your languages professionally.

Marketing

Marketing is such an important topic, particularly for newcomers to the industry or for those changing jobs after many years of service with one organization, that despite being addressed in part in other chapters, it requires special attention. Marketing seems to be the skill translators need the most and possess the least of. It seems that the personality which makes a good translator also happens to make a lousy marketing person.

As a freelance translator you are marketing yourself as a business providing a service. As an in-house translator, you are marketing yourself as an employee to companies that hire translators. Either way, you will have to market yourself. Your ability to do so may well determine your success in the translation profession. Also, the degree to which you are comfortable and capable of marketing may determine whether you go the freelance or the in-house route.

Some people consider marketing an ugly word, associating the practice with sleazy, deceitful tactics and techniques to gain attention, outmaneuver competitors, or gain an advantage through deception rather than hard work. Resume and credentials fraud, misrepresentation of professional experience, and overestimating one's ability as a translator all happen. But be warned: the translation profession is a relatively tightly knit community. If you gain a reputation as deceptive or manipulative, it will haunt you for the rest of your career. Translators are after all in the business of communicating, are fully accustomed to using the Web in all its forms to exchange information, and are capable of doing so in at least two languages. Your reputation will precede you, so protect and nurture it.

Furthermore, it is quite possible to market yourself successfully without any manner of deceit or deception. Simply have something real, meaningful, and interesting to say about yourself. Ironically, the people who go through the most training to become translators tend to be the least willing to brag, exaggerate, or otherwise misrepresent their ability. They, and I know this from my experience, have endured one or two years of brutal criticism and even verbal abuse from instructors bent on showing them everything wrong with their work, and sometimes telling them that they simply cannot ever expect to translate. Ego repair is a common post-graduation practice for these people. It is instead the people with little training or experience who tend to do the most exaggerating on resumes and in interviews. I strongly suggest you avoid this, since your real ability will rapidly be revealed as you actually translate on a daily basis, and you may lose not only your credibility and job, but also any future prospects as a translator.

Basic Marketing

The most overlooked piece of advice regarding marketing is that you actually have to do it. Marketing does not happen by itself, it cannot be automated, nor left as a minor task to attend to once a week or twice a month. Marketing is a part of business, and for the freelance translator or interpreter, it becomes a part of your job responsibilities.

This seems obvious, but I often hear from translators and interpreters who lament their lack of work while saying that their marketing consists of sending out a few resumes per month, or having joined a professional association or registered with an online group.

This is all potentially useful, but hardly sufficient to ensure success. So at the risk of sounding pedantic, marketing must be a constant campaign, an integral part of your business process, and a regular activity in your business day.

First, to market yourself, you need to know yourself. Here I mean you must know specifically what you are capable of offering, what services you can perform, and what organizations are most likely to need you. No sense in sending your credentials or calling a human resources department in a hospital if you are a translator with an aerospace background. So think hard, but not very long, about your languages, your subject specialties, your credentials and experience. This should make your niche relatively apparent. You need to know:

- Languages you can translate in
- Subjects you are comfortable with

- Computer skills, particularly word processing and MAT
- Experience, especially with well-known organizations
- Credentials: diplomas, certifications, and accreditations

For newcomers to the profession, you will have only your languages and whatever academic training you went through. But even here academic training has focus: you may have taken electives in one area, or done a thesis on a particular topic, or had an internship with a certain organization. All of this represents subject knowledge, and should guide your initial foray into the industry.

You also need to have certain skills, specifically the ability to use a computer well. In particular, you need to know Microsoft Word very thoroughly, as well as have some competence with Excel and PowerPoint. Many translators will have to use Machine-Assisted Translation (MAT) tools like Trados, SDL, WordFast, or Catalyst, so make certain you have these skills.

So, for example, let's take my background. I have a B.A. in East Asian Studies with a minor in history, and my B language is Japanese. Then I earned an M.A. in Translation and Interpretation for Japanese in 1993, all the while focusing on and enjoying technical translation. My hobbies since junior high school had included computer programming and I regularly read everything scientific and technical I could get my hands on and understand. I was, in other words, a computer geek with a translation degree and a high level of proficiency in Japanese, and in 1993 that was, as luck had it, a good combination.

I sent off resumes, hundreds per month, to every translation agency in the United States, contacted project managers at the agencies that specialized in Japanese translation or technical translation, contacted software companies and localization firms, and regularly attended career fairs, business presentations, and even a couple of trade shows. I certainly recognize that luck had a lot to do with my success; I chose Japanese in college because I wanted to study a language different from the European languages I'd already seen and to go abroad for a year. My school offered two choices that fit this description: Chinese and Japanese. I was more interested in Chinese, but it didn't fit in my schedule, so I took Japanese. Pure luck, in other words. But I also put in the effort to market myself relentlessly once I had skills to offer.

Of course, each person's situation is different. Some situations are less likely to bring success than others: if your language pair is

Tamil and English and you have a thorough knowledge of taxation and finance, you should probably not expect to find much in the translation industry. That said, give it a try, because the translation industry is one gigantic collection of niche markets, and until you actually know your background, skills, and credentials, and then share them with the industry, you will not find out if there is a niche for you.

The Hunt

Once you know what you have to offer, you must identify and contact every possible organization that could make use of your services. The Web makes this a far easier process than it was back in 1993 when I finished my Master's and started my job hunt. With a few keywords in Google, Dogpile, Ask, or whatever other search engine you like, or in job sites such as Monster.com, Jobdango, or listings on Yahoo!, you can find translation agencies, translation companies, and organizations with translation needs. Further, you can take a look at the links on the book's companion web site, the Language Realm (www.languagerealm.com), to get started.

A critical trick to job hunting is telling people you are hunting. But don't waste time telling your close friends or family. Although they can occasionally be useful, their circle of friends is roughly the same as yours, so they cannot do much that you are not already doing. Better is talking to acquaintances, old college classmates, and fellow alumni; in other words people you would consider associates. Since these people run in different circles than you do, they are much more likely to produce useful leads, and studies on job hunting and marketing have time and again confirmed the validity of this strategy.

The key to the hunt is precision. Know what you can do, what you want, and who to contact. Project managers and human resources staff are very busy, and will not appreciate a resume, submitted by mail or online, from someone whose background and ability is irrelevant to their needs. Although large translation agencies and companies tend to cover most major languages in most subject fields, many smaller agencies and organizations do not. Take the time to read the firm's Web site, find out what they tend to do and not do, and submit material accordingly.

Marketing

There are several shortcuts to finding translation agencies, organizations, and companies with translation needs.

- Use ads in professional journals
- Use ads on the Web when browsing sites related to translation
- Use Yahoo!'s business directories
- Use the Yellow Pages (or local equivalent for other countries)

All of these will quickly allow you to build a list of places to contact for freelance or full-time work. Most translators and interpreters find agencies and organizations this way, and then register with them using an online database. Few agencies at this point expect or want a snail-mail submission, so only go that route if the Web site says to do so.

You have to keep track of where you have registered yourself, so either get a good personal information manager or create your own (I did the latter, geek that I am). You can keep track of the company's name, address, contact names, telephone numbers and email addresses, and even such useful information as rates they pay, how long they take to pay, what kinds of work they tend to have, and any technology requirements they expect you to meet.

Professional associations are another useful tack. Joining one of more of the many associations for translators brings several advantages for marketing.

- You are listed in their directory, often in an online and print format
- You can claim membership, which often impresses potential employers or clients
- You can attend conferences and symposiums, where useful face-to-face networking often happens
- You get a newsletter or magazine with current information about the industry, and lots of ads for organizations looking for translators

The American Translators Association is the obvious choice for people in the U.S. and Canada, and there are similar organizations in other countries and regions around the world. There are also organizations for language pairs, JAT (Japan Association for

Translators) for Japanese, for instance, and organizations for subject specializations, such as the various court interpreters groups, all of which also offer similar advantages.

Remember, you will have to do all of this regularly in order to build a stable, solid client base as a freelance translator, or to find a good in-house position with a company or organization. It may take months to find that stable full-time position with a company, and years before as a freelancer you have a stable workflow, but regular marketing and effort will pay off in the long run.

With that said, each type of organization requires a slightly different approach, so we'll look at them one at a time.

Marketing to Translation Agencies

A translation agency is a company that specializes in providing translation services to translation consumers, usually using freelance translators to get the actual translation done. Most agencies are small, having fewer than ten people on staff, and many specialize in one or a group of related languages, or one or a group of related subjects. You can find agencies that handle only Japanese, or only Asian languages, or only Spanish. You can also find agencies that deal exclusively with legal or immigration-related translation, or that specialize in marcom (marketing and communications) for a particular country or region.

The approach is simple: find agencies that fit your abilities and experience, contact them via email or through whatever Web-based registration service they may have, and then wait. I suggest not calling the agency, unless you set up a time beforehand. Agencies tend to be rather chaotic, quite busy, and often overwhelmed with project deadlines, so please do not irritate project managers or other staff with cold calls looking for work. I have this advice from several project managers at agencies, and have seen translators lose opportunities because they are considered too irritating.

Because agencies regularly change staff, you will have to keep track of your relationship with the agency, and not just with one particular project manager who knows you and your work. You will also have to keep track of the agency itself, as many go out of business after a few years, or disappear into a merger or acquisition. At the same time, new agencies spring up on a regular basis, and using the techniques outlined in the section The Hunt, you have to find them and make yourself known to them.

Further, as your skills and experience develop, you should inform any agency you work with about this. If you earn a credential, be it a certificate, diploma, or accreditation, or if you complete a course of study through a community college or distance learning program, tell them. Agencies prefer educated translators, so let them know your academic accomplishments.

Also, you have to keep the agencies you work with, or hope to work with, current with your equipment setup. When you upgrade or acquire new software, particularly MAT software, let them know.

All of this updating is often accomplished using the registration form you set up on the agency's website. You can log back into your form and add information as appropriate. Just make sure that in your records you keep a copy of any login information, such as user name or password, so that you can access your file when you need to.

If you are attempting to get an in-house position with an agency, you will have to look long and hard to find the right fit. Because agencies are small and their business activities focused, finding a good fit is a matter of patience and perseverance. Project manager positions do open up from time to time, as do editing and DTP positions, so keep a close watch on the agencies that interest you, and keep developing your skills through part-time or evening classes.

The longer you are in the translation industry, and the more credentials and experience you accrue, the easier this process becomes. Agencies automatically gravitate toward people with lots of experience and education. This is not surprising, as they are taking a risk every time they work with someone new. The best way around this when you are new to the industry is referrals. Make certain your colleagues know about you and your abilities, and get in the habit of referring work you cannot do to them under the condition that they do the same for you.

This has worked well for me, as I have several colleagues who translate from English into Japanese, whereas I translate from Japanese to English. We have each gotten jobs for the other over the years, so we have all benefited. An easy way to find such colleagues, by the way, is local professional associations, the ATA Chapters being the most obvious. Attend meetings, get to know a few people, and you have one more way to find work.

Marketing to Translation Companies

A translation company is a large organization dedicated to translating almost anything for almost anyone, as long as the project in question is large. Lionbridge is the best known and largest of the translation companies in the world. Most translation companies maintain a staff of in-house translators, so freelancers need not put too much effort into marketing to these companies.

If however you are looking for an in-house position, these organizations are among the better places to approach. But you have to go about it differently. First and foremost, you have to be flexible about where you work. The major companies are mostly located in major cities around the world, and many are outside the United States. Finding the names is easy, again use the techniques described in The Hunt, but after that, things change.

First, you have to wait for an opening that matches your skills. Realize that the listings you will see on these company's Web sites or in ads in journals or other publications represent their ideal candidate, what they desperately hope they can get, and not necessarily what they are willing to consider. So if your skills are not quite up to what the job opening describes, apply anyway. If you are close to what they want, you will be considered. And for all you know, you will be the best candidate who applies for the job.

To apply, you will need a proper resume and cover letter. Creation of each is covered in an earlier chapter, so here I will just say that each country has different, often vastly different ideas, about what should and should not, or what legally can appear on a resume. Check with local resources (Web sites on such subjects abound) to make certain your resume conforms to local standards.

If the company is interested in you, you may go through a telephone interview and testing process before a face-to-face interview. Telephone interviews are in a sense straight-forward, since you don't have to travel, dress up, worry about eye contact, body language, or sweaty palms. But make certain to prepare your voice so that you sound good. And be ready to deal with the following kinds of questions.

- What is your background, experience, or ability level?
- How did you learn to translate?
- How well can you use MS Office or MAT software?
- What kind of job are you looking for?

Also be ready to ask the company about the nature of the position you are applying for, including job duties and responsibilities, who you will be working with, what kind of material you will be working on, what technology is in use in the company, and what the company in general expects of its translators. Everything else, from salary and benefits to relocation packages and career tracks, can probably wait until the face-to-face interview.

If the phone interview is successful, you may get a translation test to take. This is the company's way of verifying that you can do what you say you can do. Timed tests are common, and email time stamps are used to ensure that no one is cheating. Take these tests seriously, but be prepared to fail a few. Every translator I've known since first joining the profession full-time in 1993 has failed at least one, if not many such tests. I've failed four that I can remember off hand.

Assuming you pass the test, then comes the face-to-face interview. This process is essentially a personality test, and according to research on the subject, the decision as to whether or not you will be hired is made within the first two minutes of the interview, often within the first ten seconds. The person interviewing you makes this decision unconsciously of course, but the decision is nonetheless made this way. So with this in mind, you can relax about the interview. Go in and be yourself.

There is useful preparation you can do beforehand though. First, research the company if you have already not done so. This is easy in the Internet age, but a few useful sources of information are often overlooked. First, blogs. Read the blogs of people who work at the company you are applying at to see what the corporate culture is like, what actually goes on daily, and maybe even some stories about interviews there. Similar information can sometimes be found in discussion groups found on Yahoo! or Google. Second, on-site scouting. Want to know what to wear to your interview? Drive over to the company around 9:00 a.m. and watch the people entering the building. That will answer your question. You may even be able to find a former classmate or colleague who is working or has worked at the company, and get information.

All this helps you prepare for your part of the interview. Assuming the company wants to hire you, you then have to decide if you want the job. So you have to interview the company through the person in the room with you. Again, you will probably make this decision quickly and intuitively, but specifics, such as salary and benefits, can often tilt a decision one way or the other.

Marketing to Publishers

Publishers represent an interesting market for freelance translators. Most do not maintain an in-house staff of translators, and so contract out to agencies or directly to freelancers as a way to get translated what they need. Translating for publishers is often a dream of many when they enter the translation profession, and this dream usually involves literary translation.

To quote Gregory Rabassa, world-renowned literary translator and author of *If This Be Treason*, "If you're not the go-getter type, you'd best be satisfied with the fact that anything unassigned you might be doing will have to be a labor of love and will provide naught but the great satisfaction of having done it". In other words, literary translation should not be done on spec, but rather when a publisher gives you the go-ahead to do the work and you have a signed contract in hand.

So setting aside the realm of literary translation, given that it is largely dominated by academics with doctorates in their respective languages, publishers are essentially similar to translation agencies. Each has its specialty, a niche in the book or magazine market they focus on, and each may have a need, at least occasionally, for a translator with your language pair.

Religious books, professional books, and children's books are among the most profitable and hence popular fields for translators to try to become involved with. Of course, competition is fierce, as these fields are well-known. What counts most for the translator is the ability to write well in the target language, to capture the meaning in the original, and to create a salable book for a new market.

Technical books are also often translated, usually by specialists in the field. The specialist may be an academic who happens to have a command of the languages needed, but often is a translator who has the background and experience in the field to do the translation well. And this is critical: publishers place high expectations on the translator of a technical book, so make certain your research skills, dictionaries and glossaries, and knowledge of the subject are up to snuff. Furthermore, it helps to have a friend or colleague working in the field, someone you can go to for answers about content in the source text and style in the target text.

Also worth noting is that the book publishing industry operates on a different set of payment standards than do translation agencies. Most publishers make payment upon completion of the entire book, despite how long this may take. Some flexibility does exist though, so make certain to address this point in any contract you sign before you start the project. Otherwise you may have to go three to six months without any income.

Translating for book publishers, something I have not personally done yet, seems like a challenging and potentially worthwhile endeavor. But since publishers are usually seeking seasoned experts for their translators, newcomers should wait before approaching this market.

Marketing to Organizations

Organizations represent any company, agency, or group that hires translators either in-house or freelance but cannot be considered a translation agency or company. Thus, organizations include the U.S. military and intelligence community, hospitals and pharmaceutical companies, financial institutions, law firms, movie subtitling agencies, and a vast array of other industries. I listed the above organizations in order of how many translators and interpreters they employ, so that those who are interested in full-time employment but not in a translation company might know where to look.

Approaching an organization is similar to approaching a translation company, but you must keep in mind that now you are dealing with people who for the most part do not know anything about translation, are not interested in foreign languages, and have little exposure or understanding of the translation process, MAT technology, or translators themselves.

Also, some of these jobs may involve responsibilities outside translation itself. Some will represent a combination of translation and interpretation, as in a job a friend of mine had with a pharmaceutical company in the 1990s, in which she was the translator and interpreter for the firm. While flying from her home to a conference where she was to interpret for her company, she was expected to complete a translation. Other jobs will combine translation with editing or project management, and still others may include terminology management or translation memory management as a job duty. A few will even combine practicing law or accounting while also translating, though this is relatively uncommon.

You need to find out as much as possible about the organization you are interested in applying to. This is the usual rule when job hunting, and it applies here. You must seem knowledgeable about the company, its products or services, its staff and history, and genuinely interested in contributing to the company's success. You also must have the skill set and personality being sought.

The advantage of working for an organization versus a translation company is that organizations have usually figured out their translation needs and are intent on keeping anyone they hire, whereas translation companies often hire on a large staff of translators, only to let them go when the business cycle dips downward, or a large client goes elsewhere. There is also, possibly, more room for advancement upward. Most translation companies are relatively flat organizations, whereas the kinds of organizations mentioned here have more of a hierarchy into which you can rise as your abilities and interests dictate. This is long-term thinking, but such thinking is often appreciated during an interview, especially when you are asked the dreaded question: "what do you see yourself doing in five year?"

A couple of points must be kept in mind with regards to translating in the military or intelligence community. First, American citizenship is typically a requirement, though exceptions made for critical need languages. Second, the application process, particularly for organizations like the FBI, CIA, and NSA can take upwards of a year, and will involve in-depth interviews and a background check which will extend to your family and friends. Further, you can be rejected at any time in the process without ever being given a reason. So think carefully before starting an application with one of these organizations, and be very patient. Don't count on getting a job immediately, which means you'll have to have steady employment for yourself while you go through the application process.

In sum, although organizations offer a different set of possibilities for translators, the approach when applying for a job or seeking contract work is similar. Do your research; know your potential employer, and prepare an outstanding resume. Then get ready for an interview, should you be granted one, and with any luck you'll have a job.

Feast and Famine

Freelance translators often refer to their industry as being feast or famine. You are either swamped with work, or starving for it. If this lifestyle does not suit you, or is incompatible with your family needs, then you should be looking for an in-house position. But the business cycle and the tendency of translation companies to lay off translators when times are tough leaves the feast or famine metaphor as still valid, but to a lesser extent, for those with full-time positions.

Either way, marketing is a part of being employed. If in-house, you have to keep an eye on your current job situation, track promotions and other forms of office politics, and pay attention to any signs of a major change in the company's situation, such as downsizing, merger, acquisition, buyout, or bankruptcy. A few months warning can give you plenty of time to secure a new position, perhaps even a better one. But if you are caught unaware, then you will be competing against all the others who did not see the change coming, and that weakens your position.

If freelance, you have to keep track of your present clients and your relationship with them, keep up to date with the market in general for your languages and subject specialty, and maintain and improve your knowledge of both the material you work on and the tools you work with. Change can happen very abruptly in the freelance world, especially if you rely on one or two clients for the brunt of your income. Many translators do this, not out of choice, but because that is the best they can do. It can be a risky situation, though depending on the client, can also work out quite well.

Finally, marketing is what we all have to do throughout our careers. Though the tips and techniques above only cover the basics of what is possible, they should give you a running start in the process of finding translation work, or securing better work.

The Job

The translation job is what most people who don't translate for a living think translation is all about. Translating is after all what translators do. So it's time to take a very close, thorough look at a standard translation job, dissecting it for all we can find so that you are prepared for everything that can happen when translating.

Even if you have translated a bit already, either in class or for a client or employer, there is a lot that you probably haven't seen happen yet. You can learn the way I did, that is to say the hard way, also known as the seat-of-the-pants approach, and blunder along for a year or two while you figure out what to do, or you can take advantage of my mistakes and not make them yourself.

This chapter will approach a translation job from a freelance perspective, so for those of you who are or plan on working in-house, some of the steps and problems discussed here will be irrelevant insofar as you won't have to deal with them. But being aware of them is still useful because you may find yourself working with outside contractors, managing other translators, or in the world of freelance translation one day.

All translation jobs are similar, and yet each is unique. Further, different language pairs pose particular problems, so I'll cover as much as I can without digressing too far into the details of Japanese technical translation or Arabic legal translation. Your knowledge of your languages and subject matter will take care of these specialized issues anyway, so there's no need to address them here.

When a Job Arrives

Sooner or later, some agency or company will contact you, the freelance translator, with an offer of work. This may come via telephone or e-mail. Either way, you have to begin the process of negotiating. Don't accept an assignment without first working out the terms of the job.

Before that though, you have to decide if you actually want to work for this particular organization. Such a question may seem preposterous, especially when you are first starting out as a freelance translator, but it is important to bear in mind that some translation agencies and companies are known to be easy to work with, and others aren't. Since this varies over time and with different language pairs, I can't say which are worth leaping at the opportunity to work with and which should be avoided at all costs. A bit of research online, using translation discussion groups in Yahoo! or Google, colleagues in professional associations, and even websites devoted to tracking and discussing good versus bad clients will answer the question for you.

Fortunately, most translation agencies and companies are reasonably easy to work with, so unless you have reliable information that says otherwise, listen to the project manager who is offering you work. You have to find out certain pieces of information, specifically:

- What is the nature of the job?
- When the job is due?
- How the job is to be done?
- What will you be paid?

Don't start quibbling about word rates before you confirm that you have the time and ability to do the job. If the client wants it by Monday and you're already booked for the weekend, don't launch into a long monologue about your rates. Just apologize for not being available and express your desire to work for them in the future.

Make sure you know what the job is. There may be nothing to negotiate. An agency called me and asked me to do a translation of a very detailed legal/financial report about a corporation. I declined, saying that the subject was outside my experience. Never take a job which you can't do. If you can't take a job, refer it to a colleague if you know someone who can do the job well. The agency will appreciate your effort on their behalf and remember you fondly as a valuable resource.

The agency will often have a specific deadline and will simply ask if you can do the work by then. With larger projects, however, there may be some flexibility. Then you need to know how long the assignment is. Don't be surprised if they don't know precisely. I've done translations from Japanese to English for agencies which have no Japanese speakers on their staff. Get as much information as possible and then do your best to estimate how many words the job will be. As long as you know roughly how many words you can do per day, you'll be able to tell them if you can do the job.

Next, the how. Some translations are only for in-house purposes and thus don't have to be as polished or readable as a book or manual. Other projects will be edited and proofread by the agency after you finish, and so you don't have to sweat every little detail as much. This is often the case when translators are working in a team on a large project. The agency's editors and DTP people will spend a lot of time working on the style, format, and terminology of the document before handing it to the end-client. This eases the burden on the translator, but it can also lower the word rate.

Note that "how" also includes delivery. The translator is responsible for providing the translation in the format which the agency requests, or at least a format they can work with. Moreover, there may be specific instructions concerning how the agency wants the translation done. Such instructions are particularly important when there are a lot of charts and graphs in the original, or when the agency will be taking your translation, merging it with the work of others and then desktop-publishing it. Follow the instructions you receive exactly and don't hesitate to contact the agency if you have questions.

You may even receive a template for your word processor, or a sample document to refer to. Always use these. The agency provides them to meet the demands of their client, and your work will be unsatisfactory if you don't use the material. The same holds for any glossaries, terminology lists, translation memories, or other reference material you receive.

Always ask about the purpose of the translation and the intended audience. Also, get any and all details concerning style and formatting before you start translating. If the source text has charts, tables, or graphs in it, find out what to do with them before you begin to scribble all over the original. And find out if you are supposed to be formatting the translation or simply preparing a text file. Naturally, you can charge a little more for the former.

Next, confirm that you can use and retain a copy of the source document. This seems like common sense, but occasionally you'll find that after you finish a translation job, the agency will ask for the original material back. You may do your translations without ever making a single mark on the source document, but most people do not. So either confirm that you can keep the material, which you should for legal purposes anyway, as well as possible reference or use for later work, or make copies of the material so that you can return the agency's original copy in pristine condition.

Of course, the above does not apply if you receive your material in electronic format, as most of us do these days. But there are still plenty of jobs out there that come in as printed documents, and you need to find out what you are allowed to do with them. Also, some agencies, for reasons of secrecy, will ask you to destroy all printed material and delete all electronic files of the work you have done once you complete it. I did a six-month project for a client that insisted I retain no copies of any of the work I did, neither printed nor electronic, and return the printed source documents as soon as I finished the job. This is rare, but it does happen. I have a good paper shredder, the type that produces little chits of paper and not strips, and my clients like hearing that I can physically destroy material when they want me to.

Negotiating the Rate

Money comes last when negotiating. In many cases, the agency will say: We will pay you this much money; take it or leave it, or something to that effect. In other cases, they will ask you want you charge. Make sure you know what your rates are. Uncertainty about money sounds unprofessional. Tell the agency how much you want and then let them decide if your rate is acceptable. They might make a counter offer and then you can accept or decline.

There are, in my opinion, three factors when deciding the actual rate for a job. First: your general rates. Second: the nature and difficulty of the job. Third: the size of the job.

General rates vary from language to language and from country to country. There are no universal rates for all languages simply because some languages are harder to translate than others. As well, some languages are in greater demand than others. If you are uncertain of what to charge, you can check the rates surveys available online or ask a fellow translator what rates for your language pair are in general. Many translators are reluctant to discuss their rates in detail, but the anonymity of the Internet makes such discussions possible. If you are taking on a job with considerable DTP or similar work, check the current rates from the

National Writers' Union, which publishes lists in its books and other sources.

Second, the nature of the job. If someone wants me to translate chip specifications that were scrawled out by a drunken engineer on cocktail napkins, I'll charge a lot simply because of the sheer difficulty of working with such material. On the other hand, an everyday business letter nicely printed with little in terms of content or style won't cost my clients much. If a client requests a translation of a medical journal article on a new drug protocol for deep vein thrombosis, I'll charge a lot because of the time and effort the research to do the job properly will require.

Included in the nature of the job is the nature of your relationship with the client. One translator I know has what she calls the "irritation" factor. Although most clients are quite friendly, agreeable, and pleasant to work with, there are always a few that make everything difficult. A premium rate is a way to make working for such clients more comfortable; if they refuse to pay that much, then you don't lose much by not working with such clients. Conversely, for clients I really like I routinely do small jobs for free. Occasionally my long-term clients have a business card, short phrase or paragraph from a website, or other tiny document that needs to be translated quickly. I generate a lot of good-will by doing such jobs for free; and I save myself a lot of effort too, insofar as the paperwork associated with such a job can take a lot longer than the job itself. All that said, you don't want to do this too often or for jobs that are anything but tiny, lest you become the "free" translator who is only asked to work when the client wants to avoid spending money.

Last, the size of the job is important. The larger the job, the more I am inclined to accept a slightly lower rate. Security, in other words work for a period of weeks or months, is worth a lot to a freelancer in any industry. If someone gives me 300 pages of software documentation to translate, I'll gladly accept a slightly lower rate in return for the security the job represents.

There is a counter-argument to the above idea: If you accept a lower rate for a large job, the client may ask you to work at that lower rate for the next normal-sized job. This would result in a downward spiral for your rates. I disagree with this argument simply because I don't let my clients drop rates. If I accept a lower rate, for whatever reason, I make that reason very clear to the client, reminding them that the lower rate is temporary. Despite offering lower rates for very large jobs or other special circumstances over the past 12 year, my rates in general have not dropped.

In sum, you combine these three factors (or any others you care to include) and come up with a price. Then, the agency accepts or rejects it, or makes a counter offer. Assuming that you reach an agreement, you will get the job.

Doing the Translation

The first thing you have to do when you get a job, be it by fax, overnight mail, or email, is confirm that it was you expected it to be. I've received jobs which were supposed to be in Japanese but in fact were in Russian or Chinese, and I've been sent the wrong material more times than I can remember at this point. Make sure you've got what they said you should have.

Once you are certain of the material, make sure that you can translate it. In other words, confirm that you have the requisite knowledge and resources to complete the assignment within the allotted time. There is nothing agencies hate more than not getting work when they are supposed to get it. Never deliver a translation late! This is the number one complaint of clients. If after looking at the assignment, you think you won't be able to do it within the time frame, call the agency and tell them. They may revise the schedule, or ask you to do only part of the job. But part of a job done properly and on time is infinitely better than all of it done late or incorrectly.

Often the agency won't be able to tell you how long the material is. Remember that just because they send you a job in Chinese doesn't mean that anyone there actually reads the language. If they can't give you an estimate, tell them that you need to see all of the material before you will agree to a delivery schedule. If they don't yet have all of the material, and this can happen when they are awaiting arrival of the rest of a document from their client, then inform them firmly but politely that any estimate you give now will be subject to revision, possibly considerable revision. Agencies realize this, or will accept it once you tell them, and so will be happy to await an accurate estimate from you. Also, do not accept a page count: we all know that desktop publishing obviates the utility of a page count.

Once you have confirmed that you can do the job on time, all you have to do is do the job and then deliver it. We'll get to delivery in a moment, but before that, let's look at some of the more common issues that often arise while translating.

First, since we all work on computers, a hard disk crash, CPU failure, printer failure, disk drive failure, virus attack, and even having the computer stolen are facts of life. I know many translators, myself included, who have struggled through disasters such as these. So back up everything you do every day. If worse comes to worse, send them the disk and let them deal with it. The best reason to back up is that your work is your income; you wouldn't keep money in an unsafe place, practice the same level of paranoia with your data.

Typically, however, the problems that challenge translators are found in the source text. Such difficulties include terminology, the printed quality of the original, idioms and dialect, neologisms, and the quality of the writing in the original.

In theory, terminological problems are resolved by looking in a dictionary. But if you work in a very technical field, or if you work with creative material, you'll encounter words and phrases which have not yet been created in your target language. Discussing how to handle this with your client is your best approach. They may give you carte blanche to create your own words and then let their editors accept or reject your choices. Or they may give you a glossary to work from. Regardless of the resolution, dealing with terminology is your responsibility as a translator. Proper terminology is very important, often more so to the end-client than good style or punctuation is.

Translators, whether in-house or freelance, have to rely on a variety of sources, from dictionaries to online glossaries, to meet their terminology needs. I have a humungous technical dictionary for Japanese, several non-technical dictionaries for Japanese and English, and several reference books in English on the subjects I translate. That plus glossaries I've created (available on the Language Realm website), and other good online glossaries, meets virtually all my needs. Occasionally I have to call a client with a terminology query, and sometimes none is forthcoming. In that case, I insert a translator's note to indicate that my translation is new and uncertain.

The printed quality of the original is mostly an issue when the source text is in a language such as Chinese or Japanese, but this is always haunting translators because of that boon and bane of their existence: the fax machine. When you receive a hand-written text which was faxed from a photocopy of the fax which the end-client sent the agency, you may start to understand how hieroglyphics experts feel when they work.

Translators are well within their rights to demand (nicely) a clean, crisp, clear, coherent copy of the source text. But even so, clean copy does not guarantee that the handwriting is legible. Then your only option is to struggle along as best as you can, show the text to colleagues to see if they can help, and try to talk to the person who wrote it. If all of this fails, the agency is usually quite understanding about any illegible portions of the text. Just be sure to tell them about it and ask how they want you to annotate any illegible areas in your translation.

Idioms and dialect are one of the joys of language but one of the challenges of translation. I find that relying on native speakers is the only way to get at the heart of an idiom or dialect. I give non-native English speakers explanations about American idioms and dialects, and they in turn help me with idioms and phrases in my B language, their native languages. The Language Realm has idiom dictionaries for several languages, and links to ones in other languages, should you lack reliable native speakers, or they are not available when you need them. Of course, Web-based discussion groups for translators are another way to get an answer, so finding one that specializes in your language pair is worth the effort. Neologisms are also best handled in this manner.

I strongly suggest you keep some sort of glossary of terminology, official translations for proper names of business and government entities, and good translations of idioms, dialect, and neologisms. Whether you do this in a simple word-processing file, a more sophisticated database environment, or a dedicated terminology-management package is up to you, but do something with all that valuable information you collect. If your information is truly precise and organized, consider sharing it with other translators via a website or translation organization.

Last, the quality of writing in the original. There is an unwritten truism in translation which everyone had best remember now: the translation will never be better than the original (or in tech-talk: GIGO - garbage in, garbage out). If the original is an incoherent, illogical piece of drivel, so shall the translation be. If the source text is a brilliant piece of scholarship with great literary merit, then the translation should be the same. The point is translators cannot go above the quality of the original; to do otherwise is to step outside the role of translator and engage in a process of digesting, abstracting, gisting, or rewriting. People who employ translators should bear this in mind and decide what they want before they start the translation process.

Now, what to do when you are translating and the original is so bad that even the person who wrote it is not sure what it means? Well, my solution is generally to create an equally vague or poor statement in the translation. This may seem unfair or irresponsible, but consider what translators are paid for and what their job is. Translators render information from one language to another. They do not rewrite the original, they do not improve its style or content, they do not insert their own clever ideas or original phrases. They translate!

Of course, if a text is truly beyond comprehension, the only responsible course of action is to contact the client and leave the decision regarding whether or not to translate the material to them. You may lose a job this way, but you will likely win the confidence of the agency or company you are working with. The latter is ultimately worth far more than the former in the long run.

Finally, in terms of translating a text, most agencies do not expect their translators to be literary and linguistic geniuses. Such geniuses would be writing brilliant literary novels or pontificating on the brilliant literary work of other novelists. Agencies do expect and deserve quality work free of errors and omissions, delivered on time. Unfortunately, some translators are unwilling or unable to do so. If you distinguish yourself as a translator who can provide quality work on time, you will get more work.

So do your work well. Make sure that there are no errors, omissions, spelling or punctuation mistakes, and that you deliver your work on time in the form that the agency requested. If you do this, you will get more work. If you don't, retire now and save yourself and others a lot of grief.

Delivery

When the project is finished, you have to deliver it. Although on rare occasion you will deliver your work in person to your client, usually you will send it by e-mail. Terms of delivery should be worked out when you accept the job. When sending a file to a client, make certain to use the filename the clients asks for or to create a useful file name, such as one that consists of the job number and a short acronym to indicate the language. For instance, you might deliver your French-to-English translation of a job numbered 31415 as a file named "31415fr.doc". Do not compress, encode, or encrypt a file unless a client specifically asks you to. You do not want to make receiving the file difficult. And remember that some email systems impose limits on the size of attachments. If you are delivering a truly monstrous job, you may have to break the file into smaller chunks, and then send each chunk attached to its own e-mail message.

The largest job I ever translated was 70 MB in size. I received the job on a CD-ROM sent to me by overnight mail. Much of this massive file consisted of graphics, of course, and not text, but since the graphics were embedded in the text, the entire document was 70 MB. At the time, no email service would accept a file more than 10 MB in size, so I suggested to my client three possibilities: break the file into smaller chunks, let me upload the file to their FTP site or via a direct modem-to-modem connection, or let me strip out the graphics and deliver the file, with them adding the graphics back. The client chose to have me strip out the graphics, but it was their choice, and that's the important point. Don't make major decisions about what is in effect someone else's property: you want to make your employer happy, so ask.

Along with the assignment you have to provide the agency with an invoice. Some agencies will specify exactly what they want on the invoice, but most don't. If you create your own invoice, you should always include the following:

- Your full name, address, and other contact information
- Company name (if you have one)
- Date of the invoice
- Job number (the agency's if you got one from them, otherwise your own)
- Name and full address of the agency
- Name of the project manager
- A description of the job
- The details of the amount invoiced

If you are being paid by the word, specify the word rate, how many words there are, and the total. If you are being paid a set project fee, specify that. Never round off a word count, and always follow the client's preference for source versus target language counts. Finally, always keep a copy of the invoice for your records.

Job delivery is a great time to distinguish yourself as a translator. You can submit your work a bit early, if possible, and truly impress your clients. Always attempt to be a bit early, if only to allow for problems on the Internet or with your file. Always include a thank-you note in email, expressing your gratitude for the opportunity to work with the client and your desire for future work. Include any pertinent information about the job with this email. Project managers tend to be overwhelmed with work, handling the crises that incompetent translators and demanding end-clients create, and trying to keep their jobs on schedule. The easier you make life for your project managers, the more likely they will be to choose you for the next translation job they have.

Money

Ultimately, business is about money, specifically profit. Business without profit is like dinner without food; it just doesn't work. There are, therefore, only two rules in business:

- Get money as soon as possible
- Keep money for as long as possible

Unfortunately, translators are on the receiving end of the rules; in other words, you want money from other people, but you aren't giving money to other people, unless you count your rent/mortgage, utilities, or car payments. So you may have to wait some time before an agency actually pays you.

Of course, first you have to submit an invoice. Some agencies and companies have an automated invoicing system that you access via the Web, others provide a standard form for contractors to use, and yet others expect you to generate your own invoice. If you have to create an invoice of your own, either use software such as QuickBooks to manage your business accounts and create invoices, or build one of your own in a word processor. Many include nice templates as a starting point.

Too many freelance translators have difficulty managing this step of the process. I know several who have been puzzled by lack of payment from a client, at least until I asked them if they had submitted an invoice. I know one translator/interpreter who does not want to go freelance simply because he feels he can't manage the invoicing and bookkeeping aspects of running a business. So don't fall into this trap. You will not be paid unless and until you submit an invoice. Make submitting that invoice an integral step in finishing the job. I always submit my invoices with the completed translation, and have found that the little discipline it takes to do that is rewarded with rapid payment, and appreciation from project managers whose email inboxes are simply overflowing.

After submitting your invoice, you wait. You and your client should have agreed to payment terms before starting the job, so you should know how long you have to wait. Some clients pay quickly, within weeks even, others take two or three months. Your translation agreement should stipulate exactly when the agency will pay you. The average time from invoice to check seems to be about 40 days. In other words, submit your invoice, and then forget about the money until its due date arrives.

Late Payment

Once in a while, the check will not come. Do not become frustrated. Although you may feel powerless, there is quite a bit you can do. First, remember that from the point of view of the business, one month is nothing. Many corporations do not settle bills for 90 days, so the agency might be waiting to get paid long after they pay you. Therefore, my rule of thumb is 60 days, unless the agency specifically states something different.

Let's say Joe's Translations contracts with you for a 10,000 word assignment at $0.10 per word and says that they will pay you 45 days after you submit the invoice. You finish the work on August 1 and submit the invoice and then wait until September 14. No money shows up. Now what?

First, there are a host of reasons why the check didn't get to you by the 14th. For instance, the U.S. mail service was involved in delivering it. I watched my local post office take three weeks to forward a check from my old address to my new one when I moved three blocks to the east in Monterey in 1995. Joe's Translations might cut checks on the 45th day and then send them out a day or two later. In other words, don't do anything until three or four days after the due date. You don't want to make a pest of yourself. Not yet.

After the three or four days pass, it's time for action. Send Joe's Translations a Late Notice. This can consist of either a polite reminder letter accompanied by the original invoice or a special Late Notice. Keep copies of whatever you send and make a note of when you sent it.

This will usually do the trick. I've found that nine times out of ten, the agency will call you on the day they receive the letter, apologize profusely and assure you that no harm was meant, and that you will be paid immediately. And you will, or at least I have. If you are feeling anxious about Joe's Translations, call and ask to speak to your project manager or the accounting department, and then tell the person you speak with that you are wondering about an outstanding invoice. Be calm, patient, and polite; in most cases the delay is a result of nothing more than slow mail, a bureaucratic snafu, or some other minor problem.

If you send a letter, allow three or four days for them to receive the letter and respond. If you have a good relationship with the agency or are not worried about damaging your relationship with Joe's Translations, call, ask them if they received the letter, and then ask them what to expect. Be polite and pleasant, but at the same time, demand concrete information. Sappy statements like, "Yeah, we'll get to it soon" or "Uhuh, it's in our accounting department across the street" are insufficient. You want details, the most important of which is when you will be paid.

If after the first Late Notice you still haven't received your check within the specified time, repeat the process above, but add that this is the second late notice. After you send this, contact the person in charge of money at the agency. Ideally you want to talk to the person who signs the checks. Demand immediate payment, and if the agency cannot meet that demand, negotiate a payment schedule that starts immediately and includes a surcharge for your inconvenience. This is standard business practice, and as a businessperson you are entitled to do this.

This approach will get you paid 99% of the time. If, however, Joe's Translations fails to pay you, then it is time for an ultimatum. Call them, talk to the person in charge of money, and demand to know why you have not been paid and when you will be paid. Further, state emphatically that if you are not paid within 10 days, you will do the following:

- Use a collection service such as the one the ATA offers

- Contact the Better Business Bureau
- Contact any and all professional organizations for translators
- Tell every translator you can find that Joe's Translations does not pay its translators
- Contact the State Attorney General's office where you live and where Joe's Translations is located
- Begin legal action

The threat of a collection agency, the Better Business Bureau, and legal action will in virtually every instance result in immediate full payment. You may, however, have to go through with these threats. The only disadvantage of a collection agency is that you will lose a substantial percentage of the invoice amount. Legal action, of course will cost you time and money, so these two options are best reserved until and unless absolutely necessary.

The Better Business Bureau can be very helpful in dealing with an errant agency like Joe's Translations, as can many professional organizations. Moreover, the mere threat of a boycott might scare Joe's Translations, since agencies need translators as much as translators need agencies. Notifying professional organizations for translators is also meaningful for agencies, because they do not want to develop a bad reputation.

Finally, if this section of this chapter has made you nervous, please be aware that in 14 years of full-time, freelance translation experience, I have only once not been paid, and that was for $90. Similarly, friends and colleagues of mine have lost virtually nothing over that time. It's also worth noting that I have had to resort to threats outlined above on a couple of occasions.

Now then, what if you aren't paid the right amount? Underpayment and overpayment both occasionally occur, and I have even received two checks for one job. I'll omit the lecture on business ethics and simply state that I always inform an agency if there is any discrepancy in my payment, be it to my or their advantage. Usually there is a logical explanation. The most common is the word count.

A quick discussion with your project manager or with the accounting department or bookkeeper will usually resolve any payment discrepancies. Word-processing software nowadays all seem to use the same algorithm to generate word counts so differences there rarely occur. Occasionally, a translation agency will attempt to reduce your pay with the claim that your work was substandard or inadequate. Such claims are often spurious, but may have merit. Discuss in detail with your project manager such claims, identify any errors, and if they are yours, be prepared to negotiate. This rarely happens; I have experienced it once in my entire career, so do not put much time into worrying about. Instead, focus on doing good work, keep track of your clients and the money they owe you, and make the effort to improve your skills.

How to Win Agencies and Influence Them

Why do some translators seem to have lots of work when others are twiddling their thumbs at the keyboard? Why do agencies choose certain translators over others? And how can you the translator improve your chances with the agencies? Along with all the suggestions and advice in this and the preceding chapters about being a responsible, honest professional, there are a few other things you can do.

First, keep your information current with the agencies you work with. Make certain they know that you are still active in the industry, and inform them whenever you are in a new accreditation, complete coursework in a new or relevant subject area, or acquire new technology. An occasional phone call, or in-person visit if you live nearby, are also appropriate. You can also visit them at conferences like the annual ATA Conference.

Second, get to know other translators and recommend them when you can't take a job. The agency will appreciate it and will think well of you, even though you didn't do the work (of course, this assumes that the person you recommend does a good job; don't recommend bad translators). The other translators will probably reciprocate, though if they don't, you should consider not recommending them any more. Being open and friendly about business is a good policy, to a certain point. But there is no reason for you to be nice to people who aren't nice to you. Just stop dealing with them and find people who will appreciate your openness and friendliness. Ours is a tit-for-tat industry; so let the rules benefit you.

Third, be active and involved in the industry. Keep track of the big trends, such as machine translation systems and the changing laws for independent contractors. Keep up to date with which agencies are doing what and keep in touch with the ones who might need your services. Attend conferences, workshops, seminars, and any other gathering of professional translators.

You may scoff and say that it's not important to be aware of the big issues or send out lots of letters. Nevertheless, I guarantee that it helps. Agencies want to work with serious, committed, responsible professionals. Of course, the opposite is true, too: translators want to work with professional agencies. So think about it in reverse. If you're a translator, think about how you would run an agency. If you're part of an agency, think about working as a translator. You'll understand soon enough, if you don't already.

A Translator's Home Office

Home is where your pillow is, and for a freelance translator, it's also where the desk with its attendant office equipment and dictionaries is. But what office equipment is right for a translator? Is MAT software a wise investment? Does voice input software really work? How can an office be organized and efficient when it is a part of a home? And what about keeping your business and personal lives separate?

These and other issues are the focus of this chapter. Again, this will be of particular interest to freelance translators, and for in-house translators, this chapter can be skipped unless you want to know what the other half is up to.

The idea of working from home represents something of a modern myth, a lifestyle Holy Grail that many people dream of, and if you tell people that you run a business out of your home, they will often express unabashed admiration and envy. The reality of course is different, and though there are advantages to working from home, they are arguably an equal number of disadvantages.

I have been working from home since 1993, though during that time I've gone on-site for particular jobs and have also taught courses and workshops at schools in California and Washington state. Also, I grew up watching my father work from home, so the idea of a home office, including lots of computer equipment, seems natural to me. In high school the storage room behind the garage had at one point a minicomputer in it, and at other times there were various machines around the home.

Since starting my own home office, I've learned a number of tricks that make it work well, and a number of lessons that should be useful to anyone setting up their first office. But first, the basics.

When Home Is Not Home

A home office, as defined by the Internal Revenue Service, is a space in your home reserved exclusively for your business. In other words, it is not your kitchen table with a laptop on it, nor your sun deck with a chaise lounge on which lie a computer and a source text, nor the sofa in your living room or a corner in your bedroom. Such arrangements may be where and how great businesses start, but for a business to succeed in the long run it requires focus, discipline, and dedication. Your home office will inevitably reflect this, or at least it should.

The primary requirement for a home office is that you are running a business from within it. In other words, if you are an employee of one company working from home, you are not entitled to a Business Use of Home deduction on your income taxes, though there may be other deductions for you, such as Unreimbursed Business Expenses; consult a tax professional for details. Your business has to be open and available to all who want it, and you have to conduct at least some of your business from your home office.

The IRS regulations are a bit looser these days than in the past. Your home office has to be your primary place of business, but you are allowed to conduct a substantial portion of your business activity outside of it. The tax details of having a home office will be covered later in this chapter, so for now just keep in mind that there is some paperwork you will want to do, since there are deductions to be had.

A Proper Office

Your home office ideally should be in its own room, where you have all your business equipment, records and files, and resources such as dictionaries, encyclopedias, glossaries, and reference books available. Your home office should look like an office, and it should function like an office. Although each person has a different vision of what an office should be in detail, there are certain obvious tendencies which will greatly benefit you if followed.

First, as said above, your home office should be a separate room. This not only creates a defined space for you to work in, but also allows you to separate yourself from the rest of the household when working. I can close the door to my home office. This simple feature lets you keep out family and pets if you have any, or at least serves as a signal that you are concentrating on work. The arrangement is easy to make: many married freelance translators simply ask their spouses to knock if the door is closed. Children can be a bit trickier, as knocking politely may not yet be in their behavioral vocabulary. Parents have their own styles, and children their individual personalities, so I can't say what will work best for you, but establishing and sticking to a simple system works best. Nowadays I keep an open-door policy, which means my cats wander in and out as I work, often encouraging me to take a break and play with them. This is actually a good thing for me, as I have a tendency to get too focused on my work and forget to rest my arms and eyes.

Second, you need a proper desk and chair on which to work. You will spend a lot of time at that desk and in that chair, so choose wisely. An ergonomically sound arrangement will be much more comfortable in the long run, and reduce the risk of repetitive strain injuries. The desk should be large enough for you to work comfortably at even when you have several pages of source text, a couple of books, and writing utensils scattered around. It should also have a keyboard tray, useful for comfort when typing and convenient for getting rid of the keyboard when not typing. The chair should be comfortable to sit in for hours on end. Some people recommend purchasing a very expensive, ergonomically optimized chair, while others will suggest a simpler chair augmented with pillows or foam wedges. I use the latter comfortably, preferring to customize my chair to my exact needs on that day by adjusting the pillows and foam wedges. But that's just a personal preference: some friends of mine are very happy with the more expensive, ergonomic chairs.

Third, you need some means to stack and store supplies, files and records, and reference materials. Filing cabinets and shelves are the obvious choice. Having your dictionaries and other reference materials within easy reach is vital when working hard to meet a deadline, and keeping your records, including old translations, accounting information, and taxes, organized is useful when looking for old information, or preparing invoices or current taxes. You may also find a printer stand useful, unless your desk is large enough to accommodate your printer in addition to the computer system and the translation materials you will be working on.

Fourth, you need to keep this space as an office, not only so that you can work when and how you want without interruption or interference, but also to prevent the line between your working life and personal life from blurring. People who work out of the corner of their bedroom full time usually find within a year or two that they are burnt out, unable to focus on work, uncomfortable with the prospect of work, or unwilling to take time away from work. A career is a long-term endeavor like a marathon; a proper attitude and discipline are essential for success.

Last, your home office will need some personal touches, whether a picture or poster on the wall, an appealing lamp, or something decorative on the shelves. In the same way that people decorate their cubicles at a company, you should do something that you like to your home office so that being there is not unpleasant.

The point of a properly set up home office is not only to give you space for your computer and translations, but also to create a professional work environment. Your attitude about your work will say a lot about you and the work you do. Even though your clients will never see your home office, you will, every day. A professional work environment promotes professionalism in your work. Although there are of course people who can produce brilliant translations despite disgustingly unprofessional surroundings, do not attempt to do so until and unless you are both well established as a translator and quite confident in your ability.

In the same vein, you should seriously consider dressing for work. Although there are of course freelance translators who work in their underwear or other attire that they would never go into an office in, there is a psychological mindset which comes from putting on certain types of clothing. Even though your clients will not see the clothing you are wearing, they may very well hear it in your voice when you talk to them, or perceive it in the quality of your work. Translators whose home offices are corners of their bedroom and wear a bathrobe to work generally produce lower quality work than those with a proper home office who wear reasonable clothing.

All that said, you should create your home office slowly, not all at once. When starting out as a freelance translator, your income situation will be precarious for a while, possibly months or more. Furthermore, you may discover that you do not like freelance translation. Consequently, limit your upfront investment by purchasing simple furniture from inexpensive sources with the intention to upgrade as your business flourishes. You risk less at the outset this way, and can motivate and reward yourself for your success later on.

Home Office Deductions

You can legitimately take numerous deductions for the business use of your home. Not only a percentage of the rent or mortgage payment based on the size of your office (you work out what percentage of your home is used as an office based on square footage), but the same percentage can be deducted from all your utility bills, including gas, electric, and water. Moreover, a business telephone line, or long-distance business phone calls made on your personal telephone line, is deductible. Any and all furniture purchased for the office is deductible. Equipment, such as software and hardware, is deductible (but be careful on this one, the IRS watches computer hardware and software very closely). And all supplies, including paper, pens and pencils, stamps, envelopes, fax paper, printer toner or ink, paper clips and staples, are deductible too.

The IRS asks only two things when you make these deductions. One: they are legitimate office or business needs; two: you keep meticulous records, including receipts. The latter is only important if you are audited, but considering how many self- employed people are audited every year, and I personally know many translators who have been audited, keep the receipts. You can deduct the cost of the containers they are in as well as the space they use in your home.

So if the IRS lets you deduct a percentage of the space in your apartment as a home office, then the logical thing to do is make your entire apartment or house a home office, right? Wrong. Then, you say, the logical thing to do is make the largest part of your home the office (say the living room or ball room). Not quite. Remember, it is a percentage, and the IRS computers get very suspicious of claims of 100%. Moreover, your home office percentage is checked against your profession (which you fill out in the beginning of the Schedule C) and translators, who maintain no inventory, do not meet clients on site, and require no fancy equipment, are not expected to use 600 square feet for one person. You are welcome to gamble with the ratio, but from what I understand, anything above 30% or about 200 square feet or so, the maximum size of a typical room in an apartment or normal house, is likely to get your return flagged for an audit.

Also, although it is extremely unlikely that an IRS auditor will ever visit your home office to verify your claims about your home office, you may be expected to produce floor plans or other similar documentation during an audit, as well as proof that you have the equipment, furniture, or other business assets you claim to have. If you are being reasonable about your business assets and your home office, this shouldn't arise. If you are trying to exploit the system, you are likely to be audited, and you will also likely fail any attempt to justify extravagance.

Advantages and Disadvantages

What I like most about having a home office is the commute. I can reach my place of work in a matter of seconds, and the only traffic I encounter is cats hoping to lure me to the kitchen so they can get a treat. I never have to worry about the weather, roadwork, accidents, or problems with my vehicle when going to work. Having a broken foot in the fall of 2004 did not impede or interfere with my getting to work. And of course the return home is quite quick: just go out the door and there it is.

Because of the extremely short commute, I can go to work very quickly to get small things done a client might be interested in. I occasionally get calls over the weekend and can attend to my clients' needs very conveniently. Furthermore, the office is my office, not owned or overseen by a bureaucracy nor managed or regulated by anyone other than me. I can set my rules, modify them as I want, and make changes to the equipment, furniture, or even the layout as I like.

This level of freedom can be a lot of fun, but it's also a bit of a burden. Although no one seems to enjoy a gray cubicle à la Dilbert, creating your own office from scratch is no simple task. Fortunately, the major office supply stores offer online furniture planning guides, some of which even include simple simulators to show you what your office will look like. Another issue with office furniture is assembly. No in-house translator has to assemble his own desk or printer stand; I have assembled several in the past ten years. And if something breaks, a keyboard tray for instance, you have to repair or replace it on your own time. As a business owner with one employee, yourself, you are responsible for all of this.

The most obvious downside of a home office for most people is that there is only one person in it. Many people enjoy the camaraderie, collegiality, and even the friendly competition that emerges in a group of people working together on a project in a company. They derive strength, confidence, and creativity from their peers, and benefit from the motivation and structure that comes from a competent supervisor. In other words, one of the key traits necessary to be successful in a home office is the ability to maintain your discipline even when no one is watching.

Another downside is that part of your home is sacrificed to work. Instead of a spare bedroom or den, you have an office. Every freelance translator has to make this kind of sacrifice in order to accommodate their careers. While this may not seem like a big deal, you can always rent or buy a larger place, bear in mind that you pay for the space, even though you do get some of what you pay back in the form of the Business Use of Home deduction.

Ultimately, a home office is a reflection of you and your relationship to your business. Donald Trump, a person who knows quite a bit about success in business, suggests treating your business the way you would a lover. Give your business to respect, commitment, and passion necessary for success, and your business will repay you in kind. If you cannot bring that attitude to your home office, you are very unlikely to succeed there.

Translators and Computer Technology

Here we find the core of a translator's life. Without a computer and its attendant peripherals and software, a translator cannot work in the modern translation industry. But there is a bewildering array of options out there, so many makes and models of machines, with a wide variety of equipment to connect to them and software to install on them. Here I'll boil down this problem to its essentials and give the best recommendations I can based on my experience as a technical translator and all-around geek.

Of course, we again confront the core difference of freelance versus in-house. A freelance translator has to make all the decisions regarding equipment purchases, while an in-house translator is often just given a machine and told to get to work. But in many companies, the translators are allowed, and at times even expected to inform management of what they need to be more productive, efficient, or effective. So regardless of where you are in the profession, you need to know a lot about computers and technology.

Furthermore, it's not just the technology but how you use it. Some people get a lot more out of their hardware and software than others, and you definitely want to be in the latter group. A simple upgrade can greatly enhance productivity, a new software tool can increase accuracy, a new piece of hardware can alleviate inconvenience or improve performance. Many employers are quite responsive to reasonable requests from their staff for new equipment, especially if it is inexpensive and promises productivity improvements. So in this chapter we'll look at computer hardware, software, and peripherals from these perspectives so that you can make the most of what is on your desk, whether you get to choose exactly what it is or not.

Most translators I know have little interest in technology and often prefer to avoid their computers. Translators typically come from a liberal arts background in the United States, having studying language and literature in college, usually after three or more years of their second language in high school. Similarly, in other countries where students are often tracked by interest and ability as early as junior high school, translators usually come from a language arts background, with little science or math in their education.

So there is a latent reluctance if not an outright resistance to making the most of that modern extension of the human brain: the computer. Advances in operating systems and software application interfaces, plug-and-play compatibility for hardware, and improvements in input mechanisms such as voice-input software make computer use easier than ever, and create opportunities to do more with less effort.

A computer should make your life easier by letting you focus on what you as a human being are good at and taking over for you what you would just not handle well. Humans still make much better translators than computer do, and computers handle storage, formatting, and structuring of documents better than people. So look at your computer as an opportunity to improve your work. Take the time to explore its potential. Just because you were told you were good at language, and by extension not good at math or science, doesn't mean you can't get a lot out of a computer.

The Computer

The first rule of choosing a computer is: Software determines hardware. Buy the computer that will run the software you need. So you have to figure out what software you will be using, and only then can you decide what computer to purchase. You'll spend considerably less time and money making computer decisions if you approach them this way. If you are in-house, you may not be able to choose the computer, but you can request additional memory or a larger hard drive for your machines, two changes that often greatly improve performance.

You also have to consider what you'll be doing with your computer in the next year or two. Put another way: it's better to spend a little more now than have to buy something completely new in six or twelve months. Remember that translators have to maintain their systems and upgrade constantly in order to produce the file formats being used by businesses around the world and to take advantage of any time-saving technologies. Remember, even if you don't, your competition will, and you can't survive if you are less efficient than your competition.

As a translator you will be creating and manipulating documents in a word processor, often with the assistance of Machine-Assisted Translation (MAT) software. Virtually every translation agency and company in the United States uses Microsoft Word, and many want their translators to use Trados for MAT. Since Trados only runs under Microsoft Windows, your choice for your computer is obvious: buy a PC that runs the latest version of Windows.

I realize that Apple makes many fine systems, and that Linux machines are very useful as well. I've had about a dozen Macs in the past 15 years, and have had Linux running several machines. The Mac OS is certainly more stable, streamlined, and secure than Windows, though Microsoft is steadily gaining ground. And Linux is now easier to install and run than ever, with excellent documentation and applications available. All that said, the software you need as a translator simply isn't available for these platforms, at least not as of 2006. MAT software is still written, with a couple of exceptions, for Windows only. Good voice-input software is also only available under Windows. So regardless of your feelings about Microsoft, Bill Gates, or Windows, you are going to have to use those systems.

Second rule of choosing a computer: Keep it simple. Buy your system from a major manufacturer that produces a good package deal and that will be around in one, two, or five years to provide the technical support and service you need. Unless you are quite competent with hardware configurations and software installation and maintenance (in which case you don't need my suggestions for purchasing a computer), stick to the major players in the industry: Dell, Gateway, or Hewlett Packard, among others.

Nowadays computer systems come with respectable monitors, as well as a good keyboard and mouse. In the past you had to compare and purchase these items carefully, but you can now select a system without worrying about these devices. A computer is now a commodity product, as Dell has proven with its business model and commercial success, which means you simply select a system with the specifications you need and buy it.

What specifications do you need? As of 2006, you should get a Pentium 4 machine with at least 1 GB of RAM (memory), a 160 GB hard disk, and a CD/DVD burner for backup and storage of files. Your system will come with a fax/modem, speakers, keyboard and mouse, and a monitor. I suggest you buy a larger monitor if possible. You will look at it every day for hours, and will have multiple windows open as you work on a document, search the Web for terminology, and check email, so the extra size will be put to good use.

What about laptops? A laptop may seem convenient, and certainly is if you are interpreting as well as translating and want to take your work with you, or like to do research in the library. However, you pay more for the same performance, because in the computer industry smaller means greater expense. Also, screen size is inevitably smaller, and the keyboard can be cramped. Finally, it is much easier to service or upgrade a desktop machine than a laptop. I'd therefore urge you to start with a desktop machine, and if your business requires one, then get a laptop. Many companies will give translators a laptop in addition to a desktop computer, under the assumption that the laptop will be put to business use at home. Laptops are now inexpensive enough that they are neither the status symbol nor the major expense that they once were. If you are fortunate enough to work for an employer that gives you both, excellent. Enjoy. I usually have two computers, one desktop and one laptop, though for the past couple of years have had only one computer: a desktop with a large monitor.

There is never a good or bad time to buy a computer. No matter how hard you try, a faster, more powerful machine will be available within months. I suggest you purchase a solid mid-range machine that has been on the market for a couple of months. This avoids the often initially high price of some machines and the occasional bug that exists in new equipment. Stick to mainstream vendors so that you can be confident that you'll have support for your equipment even a few years into the future, and to make selling the equipment, should you choose to do so, easier when the time comes to upgrade.

Software

The principal piece of software translators work with is of course a word processor. Most clients expect their freelance translators to have Microsoft Word, though of course some translators use WordPerfect, Star Office, or the word processor in a Works package to produce compatible output. Since Trados and other MAT packages principally or exclusively work with Microsoft Word, more and more translators find they have to have it.

This implies that translators, whether in-house or freelance, have very strong skills with MS Word. You must be able to handle not only all the obvious, basic functions of work processing, but also features such as Track Changes, Styles, creating or altering tables of contents or indices, and dealing with embedded graphics, Word Art, or tables.

Although most documents they are translated arrive in Word.doc format, some translations are done using files created in Microsoft Excel, Microsoft PowerPoint, or other packages. Depending on your clients, freelance translators may find it necessary to have Microsoft Office. There are of course other office suite packages, such as Star Office from Sun Microsystems, but for reasons of compatibility, Microsoft Office is the one most translators have and use. Although expensive if bought separately, you can save yourself a fair amount of money by buying it when you buy your computer. Most computer manufacturers will give you a significant discount at the time of purchase.

A database or personal information manager (PIM) is another valuable tool for a translator. You have to manage not only your terminology and glossaries, but also your clients and business contacts. The database can, if you put in the time, take care of all of these needs, where as a PIM package will only handle business contacts and clients. In addition, a database can also handle accounting and finance for you, or you can purchase a dedicated package such as QuickBooks, Microsoft Money, or MYOB. If you have the full version of Microsoft Office, then you have MS Access, a powerful database that can handle all of your needs.

Taxes are best handled by dedicated software such as TurboTax or TaxCut. I've been using such software without a problem since 1993 and have been very pleased with it.

Machine Assisted Translation (MAT) software is all but essential for most freelance translators today. Trados dominates the market, though Deja Vu and Catalyst offer strong products as well. Let your clients determine your needs; if no one wants you to use the software, then do not bother with the expense. If, however, the majority of your clients want it, and they probably will, then you will have to have it and learn to use it.

Voice input software now works well for business use. I've been using DragonSystem's Naturally Speaking Preferred from ScanSoft since 1999 and version 4. The current version is 9; it is quite accurate with straight-forward text. I can input over 1000 words per hour (which is far more than I can translate per hour) with perhaps one correction every other sentence or so. Bear in mind that if you plan to run voice-input software, you'll need a very fast computer

119

stuffed with RAM. Unfortunately for Macintosh users, the choices for voice input are limited and poor. Neither IBM's ViaVoice nor iListen from MacSpeech do particularly well, not, that is, good enough for professional purposes, in my view.

Games have a number of legitimate and useful purposes for a translator. One, games are a great way to break up the work day, to relax and have fun for a little while in your office. You are alone there, and may find that a quick distraction or pressure release is useful. Two, games are a great way to test a computer, new or used. Nothing taxes a computer system like a flight simulator, 3D shooter, or other visually impressive game (Minesweeper and Solitaire don't count here). You could spend days using Word before detecting a problem with your hard disk, sound card, or CD-ROM drive; with a game, it'd take all of ten minutes. Last, games are a vital part of the translation profession. Nintendo and Microsoft, among others, routinely hire translators to work on their consoles and games. Many freelance translators have worked on game manuals or screen content, myself included. Moreover, to no small degree games have driven the rise in computer capacity during the past decade. So why not be ready to make money? Play some games from time to time so that you are familiar with the language and content of a potentially very lucrative market.

Finally, a few general rules about buying software. One, don't rely exclusively on the reviews you read in magazines. They are written by underpaid, overworked computer geeks who are given five software applications and asked to figure them out, and then evaluate them and write an article in one week. Instead, use reviews to find out what's out there and how much it costs. Then talk to people who use the software. Try out the software in a store. And when you buy it, do so from a place which has a good exchange policy or money-back guarantee (unless you know you want the package). After a week of using the software, if you don't like it, return it and get something else.

Two: don't buy the biggest, most expensive, most powerful, feature-laden package available. Instead, find some modest package and get started with that. You'll save time, money and frustration. When you are ready, you can buy, or for a fraction of the cost trade up to, the more powerful package. Remember, you'll be buying software regularly over the years, upgrading your existing packages, and constantly learning how to do new and better things.

Three: read about the software you use. Local libraries usually have dozens of books on the major operating systems and common business and productivity software packages. Spend some time browsing these books, trying out the techniques, and practicing until you are comfortable with the package. These books often provide clearer, more concise explanations and examples than the manuals to come with your software, though of course you should read those, too.

Peripherals

A printer is essential for a translator, but a laser printer might not be. Inkjet printers are sufficient for many purposes nowadays, print quality and speed having improved substantially in the past few years. Also, many documents are in color nowadays, with the color representing coding of one form or another that you the translator have to follow. So a color printer is essential, and color laser printers are still a bit pricey. If however you do a great deal of printing or require very high-quality output, then a laser printer is still better. So you may end up having two printers. Either way, purchasing a printer is relatively easy nowadays. Check recent issues of *PC Magazine*, *Consumer Reports*, or online sources such as CNet.com for reviews and recommendations of current products.

A scanner is also useful. You can scan text or images into your computer, and from there fax it, e-mail it to someone, or incorporate it into something you are working on. I only occasionally use my scanner, but am very glad to have one. Some translators even use a scanner as the first step in taking a printed text and converting it to electronic format, the second step being optical character recognition using software like OmniPage. This can be useful if you want to work on all your translations in MAT software, regardless of the format you receive them in. Of course, this will only work reliably with languages written using the Roman alphabet. Although OCR exists for Japanese and other languages written in characters or scripts, is still expensive and not especially accurate. As with printers, read reviews and recommendations in order to pick the best scanner for you.

For freelancers, an all-in-one printer is a good option. Canon, HP, and other manufacturers all make reliable models that can print, fax, scan, and copy documents in black-and-white as well as color.

Canon is my favorite of these devices. I own a Canon Pixma MP830 that is serving all my office needs well. What I particularly like about this model is the automatic sheet feeder. I scan a lot of documents, since I want to retain copies of all the material I translate, but don't want a room full of paper that I have to keep organized, clean, and transport if I move. Instead, once a translation is done, I simply insert it into the sheet feeder, press scan, and the MP830 and its software does the rest, saving the result as a PDF file. I then put the PDF in a folder named "Source Docs 20xx" and back it up. Simple, clean, and efficient. And my closets are no longer filled with years worth of aging, sometimes smelly paper.

There are a host of other useful peripherals and secondary devices for computers. Over the years I have had various types of networks set up in my home, have used several different handheld computers, and have worked with different types of keywords and input devices. I cannot say that one has been critical to my daily work as a translator, so I will not go into any detail about them here. However, do take the time to explore the possibilities and try out anything you think will help you.

The Internet and Web

Email, the Web, online discussion groups, blogs, file-sharing services, and file transfers all represent daily activities for translators online. Fortunately, what used to be difficult, arcane, and time-consuming online is now all but instantly achieved with a graphical user interface and a mouse. A good browser can handle most of your online needs: Web browsing, e-mail, file transfers, and reading newsgroups, RSS feeds, blogs, and whatever else comes along next.. And browsers are free. So get a copy of every major browser out there, including Microsoft Internet Explorer, Netscape Navigator, Firefox, and Opera. Each has its uses and its limitations, and your own style of Web use will determine which you prefer.

Translators absolutely must be online. You need an Internet connection, preferably a high-speed connection via DSL or cable modem. Files are too big to be handled efficiently through a dial-up connection. Also, the majority of clients now contact their translators via e-mail, so the ability to quickly check your e-mail several times a day or more is important.

Because you must be online, you must protect yourself online. Install and maintain proper antivirus software, a firewall, and anti-spyware software. With such software, you get what you pay for, so you will be better off in the long-run actually paying for something rather than trying to get it for free. Microsoft's recent move into Internet security software may eventually change this, but not yet.

Furthermore, create secure passwords or passphrases for all your online activity. As a translator, you know at least two languages, and have a memory that is above average. So you should be able to cook up a clever combination of letters and numbers for a password, or ingenious, long phrase for a passphrase. And, of course, never download or open e-mail or a file attachment from a source you do not recognize without first subjecting it to careful scrutiny. Prevention is the best cure for viruses and other electronic nasties.

Buying Used Equipment

Bargains abound for used computer equipment. You can find them in newspapers, on college campuses, or through Ebay on the Web. However, be careful because when you buy something used you might inherit the previous owner's problems.

When buying a used computer, make sure you test it thoroughly. Don't let the seller simply do a demonstration for you. Sit down in front of it and work for fifteen or thirty minutes. You should run the following tests. Turn on and shut down the computer a few times, making sure that it boots properly. If the computer is a Mac, you should here a crisp middle C when it boots. If you hear any other noise, don't buy the machine. Format some disks (floppies, CD-ROMs, DVDs) to test the machine's drive or drives. Open and save files to the hard disk and a floppy disk or CD, making sure that the save operation is successful. Copy files to and from a floppy disk or CD. Check the keyboard carefully to make sure there are no dead or sticky keys. Check the monitor carefully to make sure the display is crisp and clear and that there are no dead pixels. Test the mouse, making sure that it tracks properly and responds to clicks. Test the computer's ability to print and connect to the Internet. And, have the computer make some sounds, be it through a game or a regular program, to make sure that the sound functions are working normally.

Many computers come with diagnostic tools pre-installed. If you can find such a tool on the machine you are interested in and are comfortable using it, do so. It will take a little while to run all the tests, but the results will be very useful. If the owner refuses to let you do this, don't buy the machine.

Don't buy used software unless you know it's what you want and you get all the manuals, registration forms, and other documentation. You should have the person who is selling the software write a letter to the manufacturer informing them of the transfer of ownership, but some software companies won't recognize this and refuse to support software purchased from a previous owner.

Whenever you buy something used, create an invoice and make sure you and the seller both get signed copies. The invoice should include your name and address, the seller's name and address, the date, a description of the purchase and the price. You may also want to add a clause that states you can return the equipment within a certain number of days should it prove defective. This invoice will serve as a receipt for your tax records, and as a proof of purchase if a problem with your new acquisition arises.

The Whole Is Greater Than Its Parts

So, you have all this advice about computer hardware and software, and you're asking yourself, should I bother to take it to heart and use it? The answer is, of course, yes. The reason is that a computer system is more than the sum of its parts. It's how you get work done. If the system lets you work fast and efficiently, helps you avoid problems and handle emergencies, and is comfortable, then work becomes easier.

But it's up to you to take the time to learn to use the hardware and software. Whether you work in-house or freelance, you need these skills, and you need most of them before you get your first job. So get to work, or rather play. Experiment by trying out different tasks in MS Word or Excel, or with QuickBooks or TurboTax. See what you can do, and see what you can learn by checking the Help menu, reading books about the software, or going through the myriad of online tutorials available for such software.

Although a good computer system does not guarantee business success, most of the really successful freelancers (in any field) have good systems and take advantage of them. Learn as much as you can about your computer and the software on it. Take classes, study how-to books and guides, check out Web sites on specific software tools. You can even ask engineers or geeks for help. But never let a geek get a hold of your keyboard or mouse. The geek will work so quickly that you won't learn anything. Force this geek to tell you what to do and let you actually do it. You will learn a lot more a lot faster that way, someday perhaps even joining the ranks of geekdom yourself.

Money and Finances

Translators, like all business professionals, have to be aware of the financial aspects of their livelihood. Although no one will ever get rich quick translating, you can make a good living, provided you manage your money. Previous chapters have discussed how to get and do translation jobs; in other words, how to do the work that results in making money. This chapter will show how to manage money, turning income into profit.

This subject is particularly relevant for freelance translators, who have to negotiate each job, or create a steady arrangement with each client. But general trends in the industry, as discussed in the first chapter, make the subject of money important for everyone in the translation profession.

Also, money is at the center of many people's career objectives, translators included. So strategies to increase income, for freelance and in-house translators alike, form a part of this chapter.

It is worth keeping in mind that, as said earlier, translation is not a good way to get rich quickly. It is instead comparable to nursing or accounting, but with one key difference. The translation profession is not regulated or standardized the way nursing or accounting are, and translators are essentially forbidden from unionizing. The reasons for this are discussed in the chapter on professional associations, but the implications are clear: translators cannot bargain collectively, strike, or otherwise organize in any meaningful fashion beyond professional associations like the ATA.

Increasing Income

Whether translators are paid for their work by the word, the page, or the project, the act of translating something from one language to another is how they earn their living. Some translators also edit or proofread translations, write abstracts or language analyses, develop translation memories, localize products, or provide other language-oriented services. Still others teach the languages they know or even translation itself. And doubtlessly some do work wholly unrelated to translation.

All of this money which is coming in sits on the black side of your financial balance sheet, and must exceed what is on the red side to represent a profit, and therefore a living. If your translation business is not showing a profit, if your expenses exceed your income, you are in trouble. Although expenses tend to rise to meet income, as Cyril Parkinson observed, you have to make the effort to keep your income rising. Furthermore, freelance translators must plan for both the good and the bad times. Remember, we say that the profession is feast or famine; so enjoy the feast and don't panic over the famine. It is, after all, the way of the jungle.

There are numerous ways to increase what appears on the back side. The easiest is to do more work. This is a nice idea, but given that there are only 168 hours in a week and 1440 minutes in a day (8765.24 hours in a year, 525940 minutes, give or take for a sidereal versus solar year), you can readily see that there is an upper limit to how much work you can do. Assuming you have as much work as you are capable of or willing to do, or something close to that level, the trick is to get as much money as possible for your work. In other words: Learn to negotiate better rates.

As discussed in the first chapter, annual income for a freelancer is the product of words translated per year times the average word rate for that year. Increasing both is the key to greater financial success in translation for freelancers. Thus, negotiations are a vital aspect of your business relations with translation agencies and companies, or any other client. A little math makes this clear. For a 10,000 word translation, if you work at ten cents per word, you'll make $1000; at eleven cents per word, you'll make $1100, and so on. In other words, you should think of your word rate as your salary ratio. If the average word rate for your language combination drops by 10%, you'll effectively take a 10% cut in salary. Of course, the opposite is also true.

For in-house translators, the situation is different. Most in-house translators are paid an annual salary, though some are paid by the hour. In either case, negotiation when accepting the job and during performance reviews is vital to increasing income. To prove you are worth more now than before, you have to hone your translation skills and add other skills, be they managerial, technical, or linguistic. Also, few companies are willing to pay a translator above $60,000 per year, and most don't pay above $55,000. These salaries are not expected to change in the foreseeable future, so if your own financial goals include income beyond this level, you will have to add more skills, possibly even move away from being a translator and become a manager at a large translation company. An MBA would be a good idea for anyone considering that route.

Rates

Since freelance translators are paid by the word, you have to know what word rate you are willing to accept for a job. Work this out ahead of time and stick to it. You might even keep a chart on your desk, telling you for example that you will do general material for $0.09/word, technical for $0.10/word and rush jobs for $0.13/word (these are just examples, not recommendations). You might also have a chart worked out for how you adjust your rate based on the size of the job. I regularly accept a slightly lower rate for jobs which exceed two weeks in duration. Make sure your rates are reasonable; there's no point in asking for twice the market average, because you'll quickly find you have no work. There are lots of good translators out there waiting to replace you; don't give anyone a reason not to work with you.

You can find out roughly what other translators are charging for similar work by checking on-line resources such as the rates survey on Aquarius. You can also ask people in local translation societies, and even consult with your more reputable and honest clients. Charging too high a rate has obvious drawbacks, but charging too little, to some people's surprise, is also problematic. Consider this: You know what a reasonable price for a gallon of milk or gasoline, or what a music CD or paperback book sells for. If you found a store that sold a gallon of milk for $0.39, a new music CD from a popular group for $2.59, or a new paperback for $0.49, you might be happy, but you might also be nervous. Why the big discrepancy in prices? How can the store afford to sell these products at prices that are way below wholesale? The same attitude should permeate your pricing. One project manager told me that at her agency, rates that are more than 10% below market norms are seen as dubious or suspicious, making her wonder about the quality of the work she'll receive. So know the going rates for the kind of work you do, figure out an acceptable range for yourself, and then memorize those numbers so that you can negotiate with confidence.

The matter of rates for freelance translators is complicated by the ATA's position on the subject. The ATA expressly forbids its members from discussing word rates with anyone under any circumstances. The reasons have to do with the ATA's efforts in the early 1990s to set a list of reasonable rates for various types of translations as guidelines for translators and translation companies and agencies. This act was seen by the U.S. Department of Justice as a move toward creating a monopoly and restraint of fair trade, so the ATA was threatened with lawsuits that imperiled its existence, and remains under this threat to this day.

However, individual translators, ATA members or not, often do discuss rates, usually quietly and outside of earshot of the ATA leadership. After all, how can an industry function if no one know who is being paid what amount for what kind of work? Further, it is well known that the U.S. government is the world's largest employer of translators, so the Department of Justice's motivations may have been self-serving. In any event, if you find that little information is readily available about rates for your language pair and subject area, don't be surprised. Just dig a little deeper, attend a meeting of a local translator's group or ATA chapter organization, ask a project manager at an agency you feel comfortable with, or just take what agencies offer, since their offers are generally reasonable.

Stick to your rates once you establish them. If you constantly let yourself be talked down, you are effectively cheapening yourself, and by extension, other translators and the profession as a whole. People value what they pay a lot for. And people are willing to pay a fair price for what they value. Part of that sense of value and price comes from the quality and nature of the work. Part of that sense comes from the pride and professionalism of the practitioners. If you show no pride or professionalism, you will lose, and by extension, the entire profession will lose.

There are, however, some times when you will want or be forced to change your rates. Any time an event causes a sudden change in demand for a language pair, whether that event is a war, political or social turmoil, a natural disaster or economic crisis, or an upsurge in a new industry, rates will change.

For instance, the advent of online auction sites for translation, such as Proz and Translators' Café, has created downward price pressure on rates for some language pairs. Translators from all over the world can bid on jobs, and consequently the translators whose costs are the lowest can easily underbid everyone else. Of course, many agencies have discovered that the lowest price often comes with the lowest quality, thus proving that a good translator has a certain value. However, such sites have nonetheless contributed to the flattening or even reduction in rates seen over the past 10 years.

Another factor reducing rates is Machine Assisted Translation (MAT) software. If the software does the work, agencies reason, then the translator should not be paid as much. Some translators refuse to inform agencies of whether or not they use such software, for fear of seeing their rates fall. Other translators negotiate carefully, making certain they are paid well for the work they do and measuring accurately the work for software does. Because the software gives translators access to larger projects, it could help translators create stability in their business. So although such software does in one sense reduce rates, it can at the same time actually improve the overall business picture for a translator.

The final issue with rates is when to raise them. You should do this very carefully and very infrequently. Once you have a good working relationship with a translation agency or company, if the rates you are being paid are within the market norm, then don't push it. Just stick with those rates and learn to translate more words per week. However, if you have a good working relationship with a client that lasts for years, you are then in a position to ask for a small increase, usually $0.01 per word. I've done this many times with long-term clients, usually waiting three to four years between each request, and have usually gotten what I asked for. It never hurts to ask nicely, though it may hurt if your request is rejected, if done at the right time, there's a good chance you'll get your rate increase.

Salary negotiations are different, and so for in-house translators the approach to increasing income is also different. Most companies have a scheduled performance review, often once per year, and at that time your performance, combined with any argument you can make for yourself and the company's general policies and recent overall success, will determine what if any raise you get. But again, you have to ask, or you will not receive. Also worth noting here: many companies give bonuses, at least when times are good, to their employees, including translators, something that never happens to freelancers.

Taxes

Taxes for in-house translators are as simple or complex as they are for any other employee in a company. So there is little on this subject for an in-house translator to worry about or even know. For freelance and in-house translators alike, I strongly recommend using one of the tax preparation software packages available. The process is so much faster, more efficient, and simple that you are punishing yourself by not using this software. If you use the same software over several years, the software becomes even more useful, as it will fill in all the basic information automatically, asking you to confirm it. The software can also log into a variety of financial institutions to collect investment and interest information for that part of your return, and can even, in some cases, automate the input of W-2 statements. Finally, the software produces clean, typed returns that are free of arithmetical errors, and so are much less likely to be flagged for an audit.

For freelance translators, the software also helps manage the process of filing all the necessary paperwork for a business, including a Schedule C for Profit or Loss, and the various other schedules necessary for business expenses and deductions, retirement programs. This is great stuff, and very affordable. It's also deductible as a business expense for freelance translators.

Like all self-employed people, freelance translators have to pay quarterly estimated taxes, as well as the traditional annual taxes. Remember that when you work for someone else, you have taxes removed from your paycheck. Because freelance translators are independent contractors, they receive all the money owed to them with nothing withheld, and then have to make quarterly payments to the IRS, as well as their state government if that government collects state income taxes.

The trick with quarterly payments is to pay as little as possible without incurring a penalty at the end of the year. If you pay nothing or very little, you may end up owing not only a large tax bill at the end of the year, but a penalty for underpayment as well. Unfortunately, there is no easy way to calculate the exact minimum, so pay more than that.

What you can do is use your prior year's tax return, then play with the numbers and see how low you can go before a penalty payment appears. This works only if you are basing your quarterly payments on your previous year's income. And it is only advantageous if you are making more than you did in the previous year, something which is difficult to predict.

If you annualize your income, then you have to be very careful with your records and paperwork. Annualizing your income means that you figure out how much you earned each quarter, and demonstrate that your quarterly payment is appropriate. For translators who have a lot of work during some parts of the year and far less during others, this is very useful because the quarterly payment reflects the amount of income in that quarter, not some predetermined amount which may be too low or too high.

Fortunately, the penalty the IRS assesses is fairly low, so much so that some translators do not bother with quarterly payments, instead choosing to use that money elsewhere, perhaps in investments, and pay their annual tax balance at the end of the tax year. I don't recommend this strategy until and unless you have a lot of extra money to handle the tax bill, understand your taxes thoroughly, know what to expect at the end of the year, and are financially disciplined in your business and personal life. For most people, making at least a modest quarterly payment is wise. I include myself amongst such people, by the way, and hope you will adopt this thinking, even if it means not "keeping money as long as you can."

A straight-forward way to get a rough estimate of your annual federal tax burden is to use the Tax Estimator from Intuit at the Quicken web site. Although you may not be able to put in exact figures until late in the year, you can at least get some idea of what to expect to pay in taxes for that year.

Deductions

The art of paying taxes seems to be the art of paying as little as possible. Deductions are how you reduce your taxable income. The key is to reduce your gross annual income as much as possible, without breaking any laws, of course. After you get done with all the obvious deductions, including dependents, mortgage interest payments, or medical expenses, you should look at deducting the maximum possible for your business.

The first trick is how to take your business equipment deductions. Instead of dealing with depreciation or amortization for your computer or other equipment, take a straight line deduction using the Section 179 deduction. The paperwork is straightforward, and because computers lose so much of their value so quickly, you lose nothing in the long run. When the time comes to replace it, donate it to a school, church, or other non-profit organization and take the deduction for the donation. If you sell any business equipment, you have to report it and pay taxes on it.

Another trick is getting all your deductions. The IRS doesn't advertise deductions, so here are most of the deductible items which apply to freelance translators.

Office supplies: This includes all paper, envelopes, pencils, pens, paper clips, staples (and stapler), light bulbs (for lights in the office), printer toner or ink, floppy disks, CDs and so on. You may say that this sounds like you are nickel-and-diming the IRS to death, but is there any reason not to? I suggest buying all your office supplies at once at the end of the year, then take the deduction. Get a receipt when you make your purchase for your records.

Utilities: I previously discussed deducting the business use of home. However, one important deduction to remember is the cost of your business phone lines, or your long-distance phone calls if you use your home's only phone line for business. Every business call can be deducted. Keep a log of the individual phone calls if you use only one phone line in your home, or keep the phone bill receipts for your business line with the rest of your business receipts, then add up the total cost for the year. If you want to be efficient, use a spreadsheet to keep track of individual calls if you use only one phone line, or use an accounting software package to keep track of your phone bills if you have one or more dedicated business lines. And remember, business calls include faxes and modem transmissions.

Advertising: I've harped on the need to market so much that it must be clear that a translator incurs advertising expenses. These expenses are deductible. If you advertise in local papers, the phone book, using a Web site, or simply market yourself by sending out mailings, you can deduct these costs. Keep records, including post office receipts.

Shipping: I regularly use Federal Express and the U.S. mail to send material to clients. The costs of shipping are deductible so keep records and take the deduction.

Travel: Some freelance translators have to visit clients, or go on-site for certain kinds of jobs. Keep a mileage log for any business driving you do, and receipts for any other forms of travel. It's all deductible.

Professional associations and continuing education: Membership in the ATA or other translators' association, or classes or workshops you take for continuing education credits or to improve your business skills are all deductible.

All of the above may sound like a nuisance to keep track of, but if you add it all up, you'll have hundreds of dollars worth of additional deductions which you can use to lower your taxable income. I use a spreadsheet in Excel to track such expenses on a yearly basis. At the end of the year, I simply print the spreadsheets, complete with summary information that Excel readily generates for me, and then enter it into my tax software.

For in-house translators, there are fewer options. The one to pay attention to is called Unreimbursed Business Expenses. It may be possible, the rules vary from year to year, to deduct business-related expenses you incur on your own, such as classes you take to improve your skills, conferences you attend, or materials you purchase. Check the rules each year to make certain you are not deducting something that will result in an audit later.

Retirement Planning

Translators should invest their money. Careful investing can yield greater rewards in the short and long run. For freelance translators, this issue is even more important because you have no employer to provide a company 401-K plan or an employee IRA to take advantage of. Instead, freelance translators can establish their own SEP-IRAs or Keogh accounts and take the appropriate deductions from their taxes, while simultaneously saving for retirement. The advantage here is that a self-employed individual can put away a lot more money per year than a company employee can making the same amount of money. The disadvantage is that the self-employed person has to provide all the funds herself, whereas the employee may get matching contributions from his employer.

Investment strategy is straightforward: keep it simple and keep it long. In other words, invest in broad-based mutual fund such as stock index funds, and hold the investments for decades. Also, check from time to time to see how your investments are doing so that you have some sense of whether or not you can retire at a given age, an idea of how much more or less you should contribute per year, and whether or not you should adjust your portfolio.

Insurance (Medical, Dental & Life)

The cost of medical insurance is a factor of self-employment no one can afford to overlook. Very basic medical coverage can cost hundreds a month for a young, unmarried individual in generally good health. Add in a spouse and children, and medical insurance costs can rapidly become a major annual expense. And as people age, insurance costs rise dramatically.

When considering the freelance path, consider these kinds of long-term costs. Freelance translators who are married and have children will find the cost of medical and dental coverage a major burden, unless their spouse can provide coverage from their employer. Moreover, such translators might also want accident or life insurance, to protect their families. This will increase the red side considerably, especially in the face of current skyrocketing premiums. Such translators might do well to find in-house work or other work where the employer picks up part or all of the insurance costs.

Availability is another issue. Each state has different kinds of insurance programs for self-employed people, and other options exist as well. For instance, Costco offers, in some states, its Executive Members who own a business access to a health insurance plan with reasonable premiums. The ATA recently announced that Mutual of Omaha is willing to work with members to help them find insurance options in their state, and the ATA is working on making insurance available to all its members. For now though, you will have to research this matter closely on your own. Asking established freelance translators in your state what they do is one way to start, and the other is to shop around using the Web.

Of course, medical insurance costs are a deductible business expense, though the deductible percentage varies from year to year. Since I started as a freelance translator, I've seen the percentage as low as 0% and as high as 100%. In other words, don't plan on a precise deduction every year for your medical insurance costs. Also, medical expenses above a set minimum can be deducted on a Schedule A (Itemized Deductions; used when you think your various personal deductions will exceed the Standard Deduction on your tax return). If this all seems complicated, just use the software

I mentioned above: it will perform the calculations for you so that you get the best deduction possible.

Even in-house translators, especially those hired on a long-term contract basis, face health insurance costs. Many companies are shifting the burden of health insurance more and more to employees, so it is possible that in a few years there will be very little difference between being self-employed and working in-house in terms of health insurance premiums.

I know there is a temptation to go without health insurance. Given the costs, it can be overwhelming, especially if you are in apparent good health. But the key word here is apparent: you don't know what is lurking inside you, ready to explode later today or tomorrow. I don't want to seem overly dramatic here, or like I'm proselytizing, but I've seen several colleagues and friends in the profession be hit with sudden, very expensive medical conditions. One woman I knew years back didn't have insurance when the stress of her job dramatically affected her entire reproductive system, and another woman I knew seemed perfectly fine until an ovarian cyst burst and she was rushed to the emergency room and admitted as a surgical candidate, later having the ovary removed. A male friend was in a major car crash, and the driver who caused the collision was not insured. So he had little to fall back on, since his own auto insurance didn't offer much coverage. I know these are extreme examples, and my own health has been relatively good overall during my time in the profession. But I also have insurance, just in case.

Your Credit Rating

Have you ever wondered about your credit rating? Just because you get lots of offers for credit cards in the mail does not mean that you have a great credit rating. And when you try to get credit to do something like purchase a house, you have to remember that those calculations are in part a function of your present and anticipated income. Since translators, particularly freelance translators, have a present income which fluctuates and no precise method to estimate their future income, credit does not necessarily come so easily, particularly for major purchases.

Imagine sitting down with a loan officer at a bank and requesting a mortgage to purchase a house. The officer asks you what you do for a living. You say you are a freelance translator. After you explain what that means, the officer asks you for income statements for the previous five or ten years. You show the officer your annual tax returns, invoice records, and investment records. The officer immediately notes the fluctuations from month to month and year to year and then asks you what you will be making in two or five or ten or twenty years. You answer as best as you can, but the officer will doubtlessly wonder.

Translators are not inherently a poor credit risk; however, their profession may make them seem that way. Therefore, you should be doing everything in your power to demonstrate that you are a great credit risk so great that people come to you and offer you money all the time. You should always pay all your bills on time. Don't wait for reminders or warnings to come in for rent or utility bills, for student loans or car payments, or for any other money you owe. Don't bounce checks. Don't ride high balances on your credit cards. Don't default on student loans or any other loan. Credit companies keep track of every bill you ever pay and check you write and evaluate your credit history based not on the 100 bills you paid on time, but the one you didn't.

We all have heard the horror stories about people whose lives are ruined by a bad credit report. What we don't hear is how a credit report affects the average person. Your car insurance rates are determined in part by your credit rating, for instance. Because of the ill-defined, nebulous, and precarious nature of the translation profession, translators should strive to have immaculate credit reports, the kinds that are carried around on gilt platters.

To improve your credit rating: have several credit cards and use them at least occasionally, paying every bill on time. Make all loan payments on time or request a forbearance. Do not use any of the low-income assistance programs available from utility companies (please understand that I recognize the need for such programs, but they don't help your credit rating). Write lots of checks and make sure they all clear. Finally, check your credit rating once every year or two, especially as you prepare to make a major purchase.

Does It Balance?

This is really two questions: the literal and figurative balance. Literally, if it doesn't balance for a freelance translator, you're out of business and have to find something else to do, be it translating in-house for a company, or a new profession. Figuratively, you can ask if all the energy and efforts justify the rewards, financial and otherwise, of being a freelance translator.

I think freelance translation is worthwhile, both figuratively and literally. If you want to know what I'll think in ten years, ask me then. For now though, I like being a freelance translator because of the freedom and control it gives me over my professional life, because I make more money than most of my in-house translator friends, and because I seem to get more interesting work. To me, that's worth the time and effort.

But much of what I just said is a matter of personality traits and the business environment. The translation profession in the United States has plenty of in-house opportunities, at least for some language pairs and subject specializations. The biggest employer of in-house translators is the federal government, and they tend to hire U.S. citizens and are interested in particular in languages like Chinese, Arabic, Farsi, and Korean. In other words, for many translators, employment with the federal government is not an option.

Which means that you may find yourself forced to be a freelance translator even though you'd rather be working in-house, or you may find yourself in-house even though you'd rather be a freelance translator. This happens when the market and your interests don't converge. Being a freelance translator of Farsi would be difficult, but getting a job with the government, relatively easy assuming you are a citizen. Japanese is an easy language to freelance in, whereas French is not. And so it goes, and it changes regularly.

Being self-employed has many advantages, as I've said in this and other chapters, and it has risks and disadvantages, too. You'll find out whether freelance or in-house translation is for you by doing it, though your financial situation, family circumstances, or market and industry forces may make the decision for you.

Professionalism

There are translators, and there are professional translators. But what is the difference? How does a translator become more professional, and enhance the level of professionalism in the industry? Little has changed in this area of the translation profession in the past five years, and recent court cases involving translators and interpreters accused of espionage, ethics violations, and deliberate mistranslation or interpretation, have highlighted the need not only for more clarity on these issues, but improvements from translators.

A constant complaint of both project managers about freelance translators and corporate managers about in-house translators is a lack of professionalism. They just aren't seeing as much of it as they would like to, and that influences their view of the entire profession, and by extension how translators are treated.

Every project manager I know has had to deal with freelancers who simply don't submit jobs on time, forget to translate the middle pages or the final page of a document, fail to follow the instructions that came with the assignment, or do not use the supplied templates, translation memories, or terminology lists. Even worse, freelancers often forget to submit invoices and then complain about lack of payment, or exaggerate their credentials and ability, and then whine when they receive little work because, in fact, they are incapable of doing the work they said they could.

Every corporate manager of translators I've spoke with has told me stories of translators who show up at work 30 minutes or more late, who take lengthy lunches off site, and who feel that 2,000 words per day is way too much to expect of them. These managers also see many of the same problems that project managers at agencies do, as described above.

I've seen this as well. Part of my translation work includes editing or proofreading translations for my clients. Often what is supposed to be a quick edit turns out to be an exercise in reconstructive surgery to repair all the damage that the so-called translator wrought, and on one occasion it was actually faster, and for the client cheaper, for me to simply translate the document as though it had never been translated.

And I've heard too many stories about translators who work late at night after they've finished their day job, evening routines, and a round or two or movies or parties with friends. Though undeniably great work is sometimes done at weird hours, for the most part the people who work at those times produce schlock. Agencies and employers want no part of such people, and if they knew about some of their translators' work habits, I suspect they'd never work with them again.

So what can we do? A lot. And that's the point of this chapter. If you want to have a career, to make translation your profession, then you have to become a professional.

The True Professional

Professional translators are applied linguists whose ability to work with language, write well, and for freelancers, to operate a business, represents their source of income. Professional translators are people dedicated to their languages and the nations, societies, and cultures which come with them. They are devoted to improving their ability to understand their source language and write in their target language. They recognize that translation is both an art and a craft, and so are committed to deepening their knowledge of the fields they translate in, and to cultivating greater facility for writing about such matters. They also have nurtured a deep respect for business ethics, aware that they are in many instances the communications conduit for a product or service, for information or opinion, and so must consider the consequences of their linguistic decisions. Finally, professional translators know that they can always improve and polish their translation ability.

Unlike the medical or legal professions, there are no precise academic or professional prerequisites to be a translator. This is a boon for talented individuals who want to get started in the translation industry and a bane for people trying to identify true professionals.

Virtually all professional translators in the United States have at least a Bachelor's degree. Often these degrees are in language studies, or some related field. However, some translators have degrees in their field of specialization and have academic language training as a college minor. Others have advanced degrees in translation itself. Still others have little if any formal academic language training, instead having learned their languages either in the home or while living abroad.

Though translators must be able to write well, few have academic training or professional experience as writers. Few translators seem to love writing; to most it is merely an inevitable aspect of translation. This is undoubtedly a cultural issue in the United States; Americans rarely respect or admire great writers, and often confuse them with great storytellers. Public school and even universities here pay little attention to the mechanics of writing, and give little time to rhetoric in written or oral form. Nevertheless, translators must be able to produce well-written material, and so professionals have to hone their ability throughout their lives.

Also important is that translators have a well developed knowledge of one or more specialized fields, such as finance, law, including patent and corporate law, computer science, medicine, or pharmaceuticals. Translators are not necessarily experts in their fields, but they do have enough knowledge to read, understand, and then translate the material. And very few translators will ever develop such in-depth knowledge in more than a few fields.

In sum, there is simply no way to identify a professional translator, one who is competent, capable, and produces quality work consistently simply by looking education or training. This makes the people who hire translators nervous, since they don't know what they are getting, and they've either been burned themselves or heard stories of others being burned by bad translators. This is a situation economists call asymmetric information: there is no easy, reliable way to figure out which translator is worth hiring or working with, and which should be avoided at all possible costs.

In other words, you have to demonstrate to a potential client or employer that you are a professional who can do good work responsibly and reliably.

Ethics

There are ethical considerations in translation, including decisions on how to charge clients, when to refuse to do a translation, or how to respond when clients or employers treat you poorly. In recognition of the importance of ethics in the industry, the ATA now requires an ethics course for its members to receive certification.

Ethics begin with privacy. Translators are often privy to secret information: the financial plans of a company, a pharmaceutical patent, or the specifications for a new computer chip. Such information can easily be exploited for profit in corporate espionage, allowing a company to save millions in R&D costs, position or price its products strategically, or avoid losses in the stock market. Translators have to keep this kind of information to themselves, regardless of whether or not they are asked to sign a nondisclosure or confidentiality agreement.

Occasionally the need for secrecy requires the translator not to talk about the job at all. I have at least two larger jobs like this per year, and while doing such work I say nothing to anyone about it other than that I currently have work. Many agencies have translators sign Non-Disclosure Agreements (NDAs) for all work, or just for some work. If you sign such an agreement, you are legally bound to abide by its contents, and you should.

The translation industry is very tightly knit and communicative; it is composed of people who know how to spread information in many languages and are used to doing so via the Web, and of people who generally like to talk about work, whether to complain, comment, or just chat. So anything you say could end up being mentioned in a chat room, at which point it would be public knowledge. And if you can't figure out why leaking the preparation for a major, multi-billion dollar lawsuit six months before it becomes public would be a problem, then you don't have the business sense to be a translator.

Next comes honoring agreements. If you as a freelance translator agree to do a job, then you have to do it. You can't just farm out your work and take a percentage without telling your clients. They have a right to know who is actually doing the work. If they decide to hire you, then they want you, not someone you know, to do the job.

Moreover, you have to do the job the way you say you will, which often means doing what the client asks. If the client provides a glossary or style sheet, follow it, regardless of your personal opinion of their word choice or formatting ideas. If they request a particular file format, provide it. If you really think something is wrong with their terminology or format choices, tell them. The client or employer always has the final word on such matters, but at the same time will usually appreciate your observations or suggestions.

Furthermore, translators should not accept assignments they don't have the time or qualifications to do. I regularly turn down work because I am too busy with other jobs or because I don't have the expertise to do the job justice. Remember, for a freelance translator, the easiest way to lose a client is to do a bad job, and for an in-house translator, the easiest way to get laid off it so door poor quality work.

Real-World Ethics

Why should you bother with such ethical behavior? What's the point? Isn't it easier, not to mention more profitable, to take advantage of opportunity regardless of legal or ethical matters? Don't we all know that success in business is inversely proportional to ethical behavior? Sure, a few get caught, like Martha Stewart or the Enron gang, but most get away with it. Why shouldn't translators do the same?

Good questions. If you actually think this way about business, you probably won't be happy as a translator, so it's not worth my trying to argue for the value of ethics. Instead, the translation industry itself tends to reward good behavior and punish bad behavior. Here's how it works.

The translation industry is a small, tightly-integrated industry in which people tend to talk a lot. Whatever reputation you develop will rapidly become known throughout the industry, and if you pay attention, you will rapidly find out the reputation of not only many other translators, but also a variety of agencies and organizations. So if you behave badly by delivering work late or doing a poor job, that will become your reputation, and no one will be willing to work with you. Similarly, an agency organization that pays poorly or treats translators badly will quickly find itself ignored. The converse also holds: good behavior, whether it is a translator doing quality work and delivering it on time or a client offering respectable rates and paying promptly, is recognized and rewarded.

Remember, you will be dealing with the same people again and again. Unless you as a translator can figure a way to make a living without working for the same agency organization twice, you will have to do good work and deliver it on time. Furthermore, if people learn that you have abused relationship with an agency or broken an agreement, you are far less likely to get more work. This system is automatic; all you as a participant have to do is pay attention and keep track. This all probably sounds familiar, and it is. This approach is known as the Tit-for-Tat Strategy in the Iterated Prisoner's Dilemma from Game Theory. It is a simple strategy that goes like this.

Always start off nice. Goodwill generally begets goodwill, and you know that you will be interacting with these individuals in the future, so there is no sense in making enemies right away. Then, be nice only if the others are nice to you. In other words, reward good behavior and encourage it to continue, and punish bad behavior and discourage it in the future. The only requirement for this strategy to work is that you keep track of what others are doing to you. Fortunately, the human brain is well-designed for this task, and there is computer software, such as Personal Information Managers (PIMs) to further simplify the task.

To be specific about the translation industry: Always start off with a nice, polite, cooperative attitude toward any new client. Trust, but verify. You can find out a lot about a potential new client by asking colleagues and doing Web searches. Unless there is sound reason to reject work from the new client, do the work properly (your form of cooperation), then monitor what happens. If you are treated well, paid promptly, and offered more work (the client's form of cooperation), of course you accept it. You cooperated, the client reciprocated, everyone is happy.

If the client screws you, screw them back (so to speak) by not accepting any more work and by reporting their behavior to everyone else in the group. Cheats cannot succeed in the long run unless the group in question is infinitely large; since there is a finite number of translators, no client can screw translators forever. This has actually happened to several agencies, some of which are still trying to recover their reputation ten years after the fact.

Conversely, no translator can translate for very long while screwing clients, because there is a finite number of clients available. Cheats may be able to succeed in the short run, but only if the rest of the group lets them. We can talk to each other about bad client experiences, just as clients talk amongst themselves about bad experiences with particular translators, not to mention the fact that project managers often move from one agency or company to another, thus taking a lot of information about translators with them. We can post accurate, precise information regarding bad behavior from clients on Web sites dedicated to such matters. In essence, we can help each other keep track of everyone's behavior, encouraging good behavior and punishing bad behavior. A translator will not last any longer without clients than a translation vendor will last without translators.

Handling Clients

The true professional knows how to conduct business, including the art of negotiation. You won't impress anyone if you hem and haw when asked questions about price or terms of delivery, or in a job interview, about your desired salary and benefits. Know your preferences by heart, know your ability and skills, and if you are a freelance translator, know what equipment you have. Give this information freely and confidently, and then watch and wait. Remember, the heart of negotiation is compromise; if the client doesn't like your terms, they'll make a counter offer. Then it's up to you to accept or make yet another counter offer.

Dickering and bickering is not the way to cultivate clients. Often a slightly lower rate in the short run leads to more work and higher rates in the future. I have started at slightly lower rates with agencies and then found in short order that they were feeding me large assignments regularly. Conversely, I've turned down rates which I thought were too low and then found that the agency later offered me work at a higher rate. If you provide quality work at a fair price, you will have clients.

Providing information is an essential part of being a professional translator. Clients have to know who you are, where you work, what you can do, and what you charge. When you receive a request for information from a client, be it a new client who has sent you a contractor's employment form or an old client requesting updated information, give it willingly and in detail.

You also have to be accessible. Make sure you are in your office, or at least near your phone, during the workday. Just because no one calls you in the morning doesn't mean you have the afternoon off. You should still be in your office. Sure, you say, but I can still go out and do things. Yes, you can. But remember that if a client can't reach you they'll send the job to someone else. At the very least, get an answering machine which lets you call in and collect your messages from another phone. Or get a cell phone for business. Also, check your email at least once an hour. Many clients are now sending out job offers via email and expect prompt responses. In particular, if you participate in any of the Web-based translation exchanges, such as Proz or Aquarius, then you should check regularly to see if someone is soliciting your services, or if your bid for a job has been successful.

After-Service

A translation job does not ends the moment you push the Send File button in your email software, fire off the fax, deposit the papers in an envelope, or complete the upload of the translated file to an FTP site or company server. To think otherwise is both unprofessional and irresponsible. Don't leave your home for the beach right after you finish a translation assignment; numerous things can go wrong after you send the job.

For instance, the agency's fax machine doesn't print your transmission clearly enough (this happens often when sending hand-written work, such as an editing job); the email doesn't arrive or the attached file is lost; the agency can't open or convert your file; the agency opens your file but gets mere gibberish (affectionately known among hackers as baud barf); the agency loses your file; or the agency has questions about what you did.

You have to stick around after you send the job, just in case. I've sent jobs in to agencies on the East Coast on Friday morning and then received calls at 6:00 p.m. my time. If you know you are going out or away for the weekend, tell the agency beforehand, preferably when you deliver the job. Make sure they know you won't be around after a particular hour and ask them to confirm that the file you sent was received and can be processed. It takes a little more effort but is well worth it; the agency will love you.

Professionals solve problems. This also means that you should try to help your clients or coworkers with problems. I have helped numerous clients troubleshoot a computer network, Web site, or software incompatibility over the phone while negotiating or discussing a job. Always be useful and helpful; it will make them remember you and think well of you.

Translators must stand by their work. Eventually, a client or manager will tell you that your translation sucks, that their bilingual five-year-old niece could have done a better job, that a lemur has superior spelling skills. Regardless of how offended or angered you are, work through the problem with the person. Ask for specific comments, such as where the errors are, what kind they are, and how many there are. If the errors are in fact your responsibility, offer to fix them immediately at no extra charge. If the errors fall into that nebulous area of style or proofreading, offer to participate in the clean-up process but stand by your work if you did what you were told. The most important thing is to work cooperatively with the other person. They have the power to give you more of less work if you are a freelancer, or affect your performance review and even lay you off if you are in-house. So it behooves you to make a positive impression no matter how negative the situation might be.

For freelance translators, even after the job is finished and the agency confirms receipt of it, keep the file on your hard drive. I have all the work I've ever done on my hard drive, with additional copies backed up to optical media. This may seem excessive, but I've worked with translation agencies that lost my translated file some five weeks after I submitted it. They were in a panic and called me, praying that I had kept the file. To their delight, I said I had it and would send it immediately. Of course, this won't happen five years later, but data storage is so cheap, and old files do sometimes have other uses, including as reference material, for translation memories, or potentially for training a machine translation system. Moreover, on rare occasions translations are subpoenaed. So keep everything, and remember to deduct the cost of the disks and the space used to store them.

Upon finishing a large job such as a book or computer manual, I usually send the agency a letter along with the finished translation and keep in contact with them as they edit my work and prepare it for publication. I also make clear that I am willing to remain involved in the process, that the agency may call me for clarifications on my work, such as choices about style or terminology, and that I am genuinely interested in the final outcome. It's always good business to be involved in the entire process, not just the small part of it which represents your work.

The Suit Does Not Make the Translator

Freelance translators are among those fortunate few who do not have to dress up for work. Conversely, translators have to sound professional at all times, regardless of the situation. In many businesses, a visual impression is the most important. A good suit, a proper haircut, a clean shave (of the legs or face), and the other professional amenities are essential to success. Translators don't have to do this unless they work in-house or meet with their clients in person. Instead, we have to rely much more on what we say, how we say it, and how we sound in order to create and maintain business relations. So good spoken language is vital, along with a confident, polished manner, and a strong sense of professionalism in what you say.

You literally cannot afford to have one of those bored, dull voices that telemarketing firms inflict on the average American daily. You can't afford to sneeze and cough throughout your business negotiations, unless desperately ill, in which case you might consider not working that day. Few people translate well while suffering from the flu and using powerful decongestants. You can't afford the cries of children, the yelping or chirping of pets, or the complaints of roommates in the background. Your home office has to sound like an office. Make sure it is in a quiet part of your home, away from the noise of a kitchen, garage, playroom, or workroom, and can be closed off from the rest of the house by a door. If you live alone, just keep the stereo or TV down, or have a remote with a mute button handy to turn off the volume when the phone rings.

So a professional translator is something of a package, combining a strong linguistic background with an interest in writing, as well as polished business skills. A sense of pride in your work combined with a commitment to your craft and the profession will bring a higher level of professionalism and prestige to reputation as a translator, which will help advance your career, and in addition, the profession itself.

MT and MAT

What do computers have in store for translators in the future? Will machine translation soon seamlessly allow people to exchange written documents or spoke words without any human intervention in the process? Or will machine assisted translation be the best that we can do? Regardless of any long term limitations, MT and MAT continue to affect translators right now, and will have an increasingly important affect on how translators work and what work there is to be done.

A translator who attended one of my workshops earlier this year told me that her boss bought her a copy of a currently popular MT tool, and was then surprised to find her typing away while translating. He asked her why she wasn't using the tool he had specially bought her, thinking no doubt that this tool would solve all the firm's translation problems once and for all. She smiled pleasantly and suggested that he have a go with it. An hour later he understood why she was still translating, and the MT software package that he had bought was sitting on the shelf.

There is a lot of hype in the world of machine translation these days. It is very similar to the hype in the 1950s and 60s, when computer scientists were predicting fully automated translation within five years, ten at the outside. Of course back then no one heard what computer scientists were saying except other computer scientists and the U.S. government, but nowadays when a senior person at Google talks about machine translation, or anything else, it is major news.

Further, the War on Terror has brought the question of translation into the media spotlight, and has also directed a lot of attention to handheld translation devices or laptops specially configured as translation systems. A little bit more digging reveals all manner of technologies claiming to minimize or eliminate the need for human translators.

The marketing hype is often spectacular, with claims of increases in productivity that cannot possibly occur in the real world. Meanwhile, most of the companies involved in machine translation,

Google is the notable exception, got started and continue to exist largely through government contracts, particularly ones that connect them with the intelligence community. The history of machine translation in the U.S. is actually closely tied to the history of the intelligence community, and several major MT companies have the CIA and NSA as their primary customers.

But there is even more here. With the advent of the Web and the continuing spread of high-speed Internet access, more and more people are communicating in ever more complex ways, through blogs, virtual communities like Second Life, and of course websites, whether personal or business.

Machine translation is therefore the next major "killer app" in the computer industry, and the company that gets it right first will likely alter the way we use the Web forever, along with changing how we communicate in a wide variety of other ways.

But the killer app is at least ten years away, say the computer scientists, futurists, and even top people at Google. And it may be far further in the future than they care to admit. Meanwhile, Machine-Assisted Translation (MAT) software is steadily becoming a daily part of most translators' work, and is rapidly evolving, offering more features for more languages.

So here we'll separate the hype from reality, and look at what translators are actually using today, what translators have to know about tomorrow, and what translators don't have to worry about at all.

Machine Translation

The perfect translation system, be it a human or machine, does not exist. Moreover, a well-trained human translator is still produces significantly better results than the most expensive, specially trained computer-based translation system. However, the gap, some would say gulf, between the two has begun to narrow. So let's start with a basic question: is it in principle possible for a machine translation system to produce results equivalent to what an expert human translator can produce?

This question is not often asked, except in certain research laboratories and amongst philosophers of artificial intelligence. This question might seem pointless, or impossible to answer. But given that developing MT systems will involve hundreds or thousands of people working for years or perhaps even decades and spending billions of dollars in the process, a little theory seems like a good idea.

The arguments against machine translation state that language is too subtle and complex for a computer to understand and translate. There are just too many variables to consider in any given sentence. Linguistic communication relies too heavily on deep context and real-world knowledge to be handled by a computer. Computers will never be fast enough or powerful enough to deal with the immense requirements of language translation. Computers will have to understand what they read in order to translate, and therefore will have to be sentient themselves, in some fashion similar to what we humans experience as self-awareness. And perhaps the most fundamental argument against machine translation lies is the claim that the human brain is capable of actions and behaviors that cannot be reduced to algorithms.

However, there is an argument for machine translation being possible in theory. It is sufficiently powerful and compelling to obviate all the above arguments. In simple terms, the argument for machine translation goes like this: "If that three-pound piece of meat in your head can do it, why not a hunk of technology?" In essence, the proof for machine translation being possible in principle is sitting in every translator's head. That three-pound pulpy grayish mass that we call the brain allows a translator to translate. A brain is an organic machine consisting of roughly one-hundred billion cells, neurons and glial cells, each with a multitude of connections to other neurons, communicating chemically with each other through synapses whose activities are modulated by neurotransmitters. Regardless of how little is actually understood about the brain, and regardless of the obvious deficiencies of my description above, the brain remains a finite object, its individual neurons can assume only two states (firing or not firing), and there is no research or even theory that demonstrates the brain cannot be modeled algorithmically. As such, the brain can be considered a machine, or if you prefer a less mechanistic metaphor, a piece of organic technology, which can in principle be understood and reproduced. Therefore, a computer that translates as well as a human translator is in principle possible.

The Real World

Although theory is important, what can actually be done in the real world is ultimately what matters. Right now, and for the foreseeable future, machine translation is only viable for certain uses with certain types of material in certain language pairs. Although a handful of companies around the world actively create and market machine translation software, it is worth noting that Microsoft and the other major players, except Google, are staying away, suggesting that the technology is just not mature enough.

But it is maturing. Systran, possibly the largest producer of MT packages, provides much of the automated online translations we see on the Web, in addition to supposedly supplying the National Security Agency with their machine translation systems. Simple automated translation software is now available for under $100 in most major languages, though the output is at best useful for getting the gist of source material, and certainly will not replace a human translator.

Many of the problem as originally predicted to delay or derail machine translation has been for the most part solved. Computers are plenty fast, and processing speed will continue to double every 18 months as per Moore's Law, giving us a computer with raw processing power equivalent to a human brain in less than two decades. Memory, in the form of RAM or hard disk space, is so cheap as to be virtually limitless for ordinary business applications. OCR is now fast and accurate, at least with alphabet-based languages, thus eliminating the problem of getting a text into a computer on the rare occasion that the document is not already available in electronic form.

Furthermore, research in the past decade has produced new, viable approaches for the difficult aspects of machine translation. Statistical modeling of natural language, large corpus-based reference databases, and improved syntax generation mean that output from today's machine translation systems is no longer so easily dismissed as useless.

Ultimately, the market decides what is good enough for the market. Professional translators often decry the low quality of machine translation systems, using such phrases as "word salad" or quoting famous stories 1950s and 60s about early U.S. government attempts to use computers to translate Russian material, the most famous of which is the English phrase "the spirit is willing but the flesh is weak" becoming "the vodka is strong but the meat is tasteless" in the machine's output. Though this story may be apocryphal, the frequency with which it is heard makes an important point. Translators are committed to making this technology prove itself before they will let themselves be replaced. They are not going to go quietly into that good night. However, machine translation nowadays already has a place in the translation industry, and its place is likely to expand.

Good Enough

Good enough means acceptable to those who want the translation. We are far from the time when the market will consider most machine translation good enough, but that day may be well within your and my lifetime. Consider this: a company wants all the specifications for an automobile translated from English into French, Spanish, German, Italian, Dutch, Portuguese, Chinese, and Japanese. The specifications total over 5,000 pages, approximately 1 million words. Assume that a translator can do 5,000 words per day (I realize this is very high, but assume it anyway). It will therefore take 200 days of work to produce the translation per language. A team of ten translators will still take 20 days, plus the time to unify the text after the translators are finished. At $0.25 per word (what the agency might charge the automobile company), the total cost per language would be $250,000. And these numbers are for each language involved. Therefore, if a machine system can translate the information at 20,000 words per hour, we see that the job might be done in a little over two days, plus clean-up time. And the computer plus software will cost considerably less, maybe $3,000 for the computer and $4,000 for the software for each language pair.

Of course, clean-up time is where a lot of debate really occurs these days. In carefully prepared documents with controlled language, well-defined subject matter, and good existing terminology references, the amount of clean-up is sufficiently small that a machine translation system can be reasonably efficient. Conversely, if the material represents colloquial language, with cultural nuances, slang, and neologisms, the output from a machine translation will be useless. Further, if the material consists of new research on very specialized cutting edge technology, the machine translation will be poor. So the problem of quality from a machine translation system remains the major issue, because the other two factors important a business, cost and speed, are where machine translation excels.

It is important to remember that the majority of material translators work on is information, ideas, or beliefs on a particular subject, and most often the material is nothing more than instructions, directions, or explanations, with a minimum of style of literary content. The material is generally bland and dry, for instance software or hardware manuals, engineering specifications, scientific or other technical research material, financial or corporate reports, fiscal analyses, clinical trial reports, patents, and so forth. Accurately rendering the subtle style of a source text is rarely an issue that translators struggle with, or even discuss much amongst themselves. So if the current human translators don't have to deal with the subtleties and nuances of well-written literary prose, then neither will the machine systems.

So for businesses considering the use of machine translation, the decision becomes a cost-benefit analysis. Although the initial cost of introducing a well-designed, and customizable machine translation systems such as is offered by Systran are still prohibitive for many businesses, those that make the initial investment often recoup it fairly quickly, given the cost of human-based translation. Further, the cost of such systems will come down, making them more accessible to the majority of businesses, and thus putting greater pressure on human translators.

At some distant point in the future, I believe, translation will be performed by machines in all but the most esoteric, obscure cases. We are at this time, however, nowhere near that point. The transition will be steady, providing many opportunities for translators and linguists to earn a living developing, testing, deploying, and supporting such systems. Humans still make much clearer, more informed, and more accurate decisions about the meaning of written language than computers do, and so will remain an important part of the translation process for the foreseeable future.

MAT

Currently, Machine Assistant Translation (MAT) is the hot topic in the translation industry, particularly in the localization field. No longer an esoteric application with a steep learning curve and little real-world value, MAT is now a part of the everyday toolset used by most translators, so much so that the translators entering the industry without the skills, and freelancers entering the industry without the actual software, are at a great disadvantage.

Products like Trados, Corel Catalyst, and Aatril Software's Deja Vu lead the MAT market at present. Each tool has its relative strengths, though Trados currently holds about 80% of the market overall. All of the tools support all major languages, including double-byte languages like Japanese and Chinese, offer terminology and glossary management tools, provide document version control, work with a variety of common document formats, and use the MMX standard for translation memories. Trados seems more focused on the localization sector, while Catalyst offers built-in features resembling machine translation, with fuzzy matches and suggestions offered to the translator to approve or reject.

This is just the beginning. Future systems will offer much more. Not only will they come with vast pools of sample translations mined from the terabytes of such material already available and extensive terminology and glossary listings, but they will also offer intelligent matching of untranslated text that far outperforms today's best 'fuzzy' guesses, real-time collaboration between non-local sites via the Internet, constant and automatic updating of sample translations and word lists via bot searches of the Web, and so forth.

The future translator will not sit at a desk with a printed copy of a text to one side of the keyboard and some dictionaries or other resources to the other. In fact many translators already work primarily if not exclusively with electronic source material and use at least some Web-based resources for terminology research.

Instead future translators will likely have a live link to their client's web site, working directly in real time with the other translators and project manager involved in the project. They will prepare the source material for 'translation' by the MAT system, then monitor the output and work on the parts that the system cannot handle. They will also perform considerable editing, proof-reading, and QA work, along with developing and maintaining glossaries, sample translation databases, and other necessary resources for the MAT system.

There are, however, several problems. The first is cost. Not only is the software itself quite expensive for freelance translators to add to their office arsenal, but also it requires more RAM, more hard disc space, and a large monitor to be used efficiently. In addition, a scanner with good OCR software is extremely useful. This whole bundle could run as much as $3000, depending on which combination of hardware and software one opts for. This is a substantial investment for a freelance translator, particularly since many translation vendors prefer to pay translators who use MAT software less than they otherwise would. In fact, some translators who use MAT go as far as not telling their clients about it so as to avoid the issue of reduced rates when using MAT. In sum, cost reduction has to become a focus for MAT, particularly for Trados, whose product is currently by far the most expensive.

Second is the question of reliability. MAT software, in particular Trados, has a reputation for being buggy, flakey, difficult to work with, and often just plain uncooperative. For technical reasons, this occurs more frequently with Chinese, Japanese, and other double-byte languages, but given how important these languages are, a product that doesn't work well with them should not be on the market. Many Japanese and Chinese translators and translation agencies and companies shy away from MAT software still, even though they see great potential for it, they also know from experience that the tool causes as many problems as it solves in many cases.

Third is the question of content rights. Freelance translators are independent contractors who translate on a work-for-hire basis. In-house employees translate on a similar basis. Neither owns the legal rights to what they produce. So if a freelance translator creates a glossary or terminology list in an MAT package while doing a translation for a client, who owns that list? If the translator cannot recycle or reuse such lists, much of the value of MAT will be lost. The same can be said for the organizations that want the translations done, too. Moreover, how would a translation vendor know if I were reusing a terminology list that I created while working for them? And should they care? Such problems are common with Internet and computer technologies. Just consider the issues surrounding MP3 if you are uncertain as to the arguments on both sides. Further, anyone who can access translation memories for a particular translation essentially has the whole translation, for free. This creates considerable problems when working on proprietary or secret material. Solutions to these problems are forthcoming, and will allow far greater collaboration between translators and sharing of resources.

In addition, the memories themselves are not reliable. Not all translators are competent translators, so whose memories do you want? How can you find out ahead of time if a translation memory is worth having? There are already firms marketing translation memories, soliciting them from translators and paying the translators royalties. But as one colleague of mine said recently, she wouldn't use the translation memories available in her company's MAT system except for those prepared by the highly educated and experienced translators. The rest were, in her words, useless garbage. So quality control, as always, is an issue.

The fourth and final problem is translators themselves. Many translators seem resistant to MAT because of the paradigm outlined above. They see translation as a highly intuitive, creative process, one which involves careful analysis of the source text, meticulous research in "quaint and curious volumes of forgotten lore," and then creative writing to formulate a target text that balances form and function. MAT takes much of this away, they believe. It is too automated, too computerized. Such translators are not necessarily Luddites; many are resisting a tendency in the industry to put speed above everything else. Translators thrive on the challenge of creating a high-quality translation; MAT is perceived by many as a way to crank out in very short times a translation of at best marginal quality. "Good enough so that we don't get sued" is how one localization manager put it. So translators are being forced to adapt, and many won't. The good people who the industry loses will be replaced by those who can accept working with MAT software. It's the way the industry is going, and there's no turning back.

The Future of MT & MAT

Because the translation profession is intimately connected with the high-tech sector, all of the rapid changes we have seen with the advent of the Web, the spread of powerful home computers, and the development of expert systems are directly impacting translators. Unfortunately, many translators have a liberal arts background with little interest in or comfort with technology. Many feel frustrated as they realize that the only path to a stable future in the translation profession involves daily use of computers with sophisticated software tools to work on the translation of generally technical material. This is how the industry is evolving, and the individual who opposes it is doomed to extinction.

That said, there are esoteric areas within the translation profession there are currently not subject to the pressures of technology. The most obvious is literary translation, typically done by university professors with doctorates in language and literature. Also, the intelligence community relies heavily on human translators for certain types of work, because the machine systems simply are not even remotely good enough. Last, original research in the sciences is often unavailable in electronic format, involves many new terms and concepts, and is not at all similar to prior material, thus making it almost immune to the benefits of MAT software.

As the MT and MAT software technologies discussed in this chapter evolve, there will be fewer areas within the translation profession that remain untouched. Translators who have not already begun the process of mastering such technology and adapting to using it on a daily basis should begin immediately. Finally, the most stable, lucrative jobs with the greatest long-term stability will go to the individuals who can not only use such system is to expedite the translation process, but can also train, evaluate, and support such systems. If you are planning on a long stint in the translation profession, these are skills you will have to develop.

Professional Associations

The major professional association for translators in the United States is the American Translators Association and its affiliated chapter organizations. Each year the ATA holds an annual conference, and each month it sends out the ATA Chronicle, a publication by and for the translation profession. Chapter organizations meet regularly, representing a local focal point for translators and others in the industry. But what do these organizations and their efforts really offer? And what else might they do?

The American Translators Association, usually called the ATA, is the largest organization for translators in this part of the world. Despite its name, the ATA is active in the field of interpretation, and welcomes corporate and educational membership, and anyone else involved in the translation or interpretation industries. The ATA provides various types of memberships, including student membership, associate membership, and active/corresponding membership. All memberships include a subscription to the monthly publication *The ATA Chronicle*.

Student membership is available if you are a full-time undergraduate or graduate student in any field, or part-time in a translation or interpretation program, or foreign-language study program. The membership is less costly, but does not give include a listing in the Directory of Translation and Interpretation Services, and is limited to four years.

Associate membership is available to anyone who wishes to join the ATA. It costs $145 per year, and gives you an entry in the ATA Directory. The difference between an Associate Member and an Active Member is that the latter has passed the ATA Certification Exam, which involves not only meeting eligibility requirements but also successfully completing the exam itself.

Within the ATA there are Divisions which provide specialized services through newsletters, seminars, and conferences. The Divisions currently include the Chinese Language Division, French Language Division, German Language Division, Interpreters

Division, Italian Language Division, Japanese Language Division, Literary Division, Medical Division, Nordic Division, Portuguese Language Division, Slavic Languages Division, Spanish Language Division, and the Translation Company Division. The only requirements for participating in a Division are ATA membership and an annual fee.

Member benefits include a listing in the ATA Directory (except for student members). This listing is valuable, particularly for freelance translators. Potential clients have to be able to find you, and the ATA Directory is one place they look when they need a new translator. Make certain you keep your listing current, and that all information is accurate. Since joining the ATA I have gotten enough business from my listing to cover the cost of membership many times over.

Additional benefits include access to business insurance services, collection/receivables management, credit card services, overnight delivery services, and web site design, along with a discount on the Annual Conference registration fees and ATA publications, including:

- International Certification Study
- Annual Translation and Interpreting Compensation Survey
- Park's Guide to Translating and Interpreting Programs in North America
- Medical Translating and Interpreting: A Resource Guide
- Programs in Translation Studies: An ATA Handbook
- Translating and Interpreting in the Federal Government
- A Consumer's Guide to Professional Translation

The ATA's web site (www.atanet.org) contains a complete list of currently available publications, along with current costs for membership. But all this said, the conference and the certification exam are the two services that most people know the ATA for.

The ATA Conference

The Annual Conference is the largest conference in the translation industry in the United States. It includes keynote speeches, presentations, seminars, workshops, business networking sessions, and a jobs fair. The various sessions are generally geared toward newcomers to the profession, and are typically specific to a language pair or a subject area. Last year's conference in Seattle, Washington, offered several general sessions for all members, introductory sessions for new members, sessions on marketing and business practices for freelance translators and on project management for in-house translators, and specific sessions on financial, legal, literary, medical, scientific and technical translation, as well as sessions on computers and translation, translation pedagogy, and a variety of meetings for specific language pairs.

What holds back some people form attending the ATA Conference is the cost. Travel expenses can be very high if the site is on the opposite side of the country, and there are also lodging expenses to consider, though the ATA provides a group rate in the hotel where the conference is held. Opinions on the value of the ATA Conference vary. It is a great opportunity to meet face to face with project managers and translation managers, to hear what senior people in business see happening in the industry, and to network with other translators working in the same languages or on the same kinds of material that you work on. It is also at times frustrating, say some, because the focus of the sessions is too general and basic, and opportunities to develop business contacts limited.

ATA Certification

The ATA exam has become more involved recently. Previously known as an accreditation exam with no eligibility requirements and only a short general passage to translate, it has become the ATA Certification Exam. To take it you first must be an ATA member and have 1) current membership in the Fédération Internationale des Traducteurs; or 2) an advanced degree of approved degree or certificate; 3) an undergraduate degree and at least two years' work experience as a translator or interpreter; or 4) no undergraduate degree and at least five years' work experience as a translator or interpreter.

The test itself is currently available into English from Arabic, Croatian, Danish, Dutch, French, German, Hungarian, Italian, Japanese, Polish, Portuguese, Russian, and Spanish, and from English into Chinese, Croatian, Dutch, Finnish, French, German, Hungarian, Italian, Japanese, Polish, Portuguese, Russian, and Spanish. It is a three-hour exam in one of the above pairs. You can use whatever reference materials you want to translate a mandatory general passage roughly 250 words long, and then a second passage of equal length you select from among two choices: one in the field of science, technology, or medicine, or the other in the field of law, business, or finance. You must pass both to become certified.

To maintain certification you must accumulate 20 hours of continuing education credits over a three-year period, with a maximum of 10 hours in any given year. Also, all newly-certified members will have to complete one hour of ethics training by either attending a workshop at the annual conference or one that is available online.

Because the ATA Certification is new, it is unclear how industry will react. Previously, the ATA accreditation exam was not given much attention except among Spanish/English translators. The exam was considered to short and simple to represent a reliable evaluation of a translator's ability. The new certification exam obviously reflects an effort to improve reliability. But because it does not test the ability of a translator to use MAT software, exploit search engines for research, or manipulate documents and databases, it is still limited in evaluating a translator's ability to function in the industry. Furthermore, the grading of the ATA test has been for many years controversial, with highly trained, competent professionals failing, and with some languages failing more people than others. So whether or not the exam actually improves reliability, and how the translation industry will treat ATA-certified translators, remains to be seen.

Perspective

The most common complaint about the ATA these days is "too little, too late." Just as the translation industry in the United States is being overwhelmed by MAT software and MT technology and drained by offshoring, outsourcing, and Web-based translation auction services, the ATA steps forward to improve translators' credibility and professional status. With salaries for in-house translators soft and rates for freelancers flat, and good job openings somewhat difficult to come by, the ATA's offering a new, more expensive path to certification and requiring either years of experience or a costly education may represent an ill-conceived step.

In addition, there is still a legacy of scandal and incompetence surrounding the ATA from the early 1990s. The organization has moved itself away from that time and the people involved, and has undertaken many worthwhile projects since, including a vast improvement to *The ATA Chronicle*, greater content in the annual ATA Conference, more business services, and it is even lobbying Congress so members can receive health insurance through the ATA. All laudable, and hopeful for the future.

Mostly though, the ATA lacks cohesion. This is not entirely its fault, however. Few people last even five years in the translation profession, and fewer still make it past the ten-year mark. So the ATA's membership is often quite green, lacking any sense of history or perspective on the profession and any ability to see or motivation to deal with long-term trends. The ATA itself does occasionally offer workshops on overall situation and trends in the translation profession, but the schools that train translators usually don't, and the ATA Chronicle does not contain a news section in which current events and long-term trends are made public, discussed, and analyzed.

Despite the above, newcomers to the profession should probably join the ATA, if only for a year or two. Of course, all translators should strive to become active productive members of the profession. Much more information about the ATA can be had from its website at www.atanet.org.

Chapter Associations

There are across the United States ATA chapters that offer newsletters, annual conferences, workshops, and seminars to members. They function as miniature versions of the ATA itself, each offering a slightly different set of benefits at a different cost. ATA membership does defray this cost in most cases.

The associations are:

- Atlanta Association of Interpreters and Translators (AAIT)
- Carolina Association of Translators and Interpreters (CATI)
- Delaware Valley Translators Association (DVTA)
- Florida Chapter of ATA (FLATA)
- Michigan Translators/Interpreters Network (MiTiN)
- Mid-America Chapter of ATA (MICATA)

- Midwest Association of Translators and Interpreters (MATI)
- National Capital Area Chapter
- New York Circle of Translators (NYCT)
- Northeast Ohio Translators Association (NOTA)
- Northern California Translators Association (NCTA)
- Northwest Translators and Interpreters Society (NOTIS)
- Southern California Area Translators and Interpreters Association (SCATIA)
- Upper Midwest Translators and Interpreters Association (UMTIA)

There are also two ATA-affiliated groups:

- Iowa Interpreters and Translators Association (IITA)
- Utah Translators and Interpreters Association (UTIA)

The chapter organizations can be a lot of fun, and are often more useful than the ATA because of their smaller size and regional focus. The NCTA can, for instance, easily serve the needs of medical or legal translators and interpreters working in the San Francisco Bay area, whereas the ATA may not be as willing to. Further, many chapter organizations have regular meetings locally, whereas the ATA Conference is annual, and often in a site far from home.

Other Groups

Every language and many subject areas have professional organizations of their own. Given the large number of such organizations, I cannot list them here. Instead, they can be found through the ATA, general Web searches, or colleagues. Their value and importance varies depending on which languages you work with and what areas you specialize in. If the successful members of the section of the translation profession you are in belong, you should strongly consider joining.

Translators have a variety of organizations to consider joining. Though none represents the perfect combination of all the features a professional organization ought to have, the ATA does a respectable job in many areas. Furthermore, it is at present the only option for a national organization.

Professional Associations

Although membership is not required for success in the translation profession, it is a way to show clients or employers that you are dedicated to your craft, committed to being an informed professional, and willing to participate in the translation industry. Membership is, in other words, one way a translator, particularly a newcomer, can prepare for or further a career in the translation profession.

Quick Answers to Common Questions

In case you haven't the time or inclination to read through all of the book, or did and now find yourself stumped as to where you saw some particular idea or suggestion, or perhaps have a specific question that you need an immediate answer to, I have assembled here some common questions and answers, many inspired by students in my courses at the Monterey Institute of International Studies or the Bellevue Community College Translation & Interpretation Institute on the translation profession, others from correspondence with professional translators and new entrants to our industry. I hope your own questions are answered in this chapter, but if not, please contact me and I will do my best to provide you with an answer.

General Business Questions

Q: How many hours per week do you work? How much vacation can you take?
A: I work roughly 35 hours per week, though that includes not just translation but also all the other business matters I have to attend to, plus study of my languages and the subjects I work in. I take about three weeks of vacation per year, including national holidays. Typically I take a week or so off in the summer and a week around New Year's, plus various days here and there that I use to create long weekends.

Q; How much money can one make as a translator?
A: The minimum is $0.00, or rather less than that, as it is possible to spend more than you earn, and therefore have net loss for a given year. On average, a starting freelance translator should expect to make less than $25,000 in the first year, though some people do manage to make more, and some less. An established freelance translator makes roughly $40,000 to $45,000 per year, from what I've heard, and some do make over $55,000. These averages,

derived from a lot of hearsay and anecdotal evidence, are merely guidelines, and will vary considerably depending on your native language, work into foreign languages pays more than work into English does in the United States in general, as well as on your subject specializations. Also, what you earn ultimately depends on your rates and how many words you can translate per day, so learn to negotiate and to translate faster.

In-house translator salaries start in the low $30s and top out around $60,000, though there are exceptions. A highly qualified, specialist translator with an in-demand language pair can make over $70,000 in the government or private sector. Achieving that level of experience and ability take years, of course.

Q: What are average market rates at present in the United States?
A: A global average might be something in the neighborhood of $0.10 per word, though this is a rough estimate that includes both into- and out-of-English translation in all subject areas. Obviously, a translator working from English into Japanese doing highly technical work and providing DTP and other ancillary services for direct clients can earn a great deal more per word. On the other end, a translator working from Spanish into English on material for the U.S. government would be paid a lot less.

Q: What is the average income for a translator in the U.S.?
A: Roughly $40,000, if you include the highly-paid specialists with decades of experience in exotic languages and the newcomers doing basic work in common languages. The ATA does an annual income survey of its membership, the results of which are discussed in the first chapter.

Q: I hear stories of translators making $125,000 or more per year. What's the deal?
A: First, people tend to exaggerate about two things in life: money and sex. They usually claim to have or get more of both than they really do. That said, I suggest you adjust any claims you hear downward by 10% or so, then consider the difference between gross and net income. For a technical translator working from English to languages like German, Chinese, or Japanese for direct clients, providing editing, proofreading, DTP, and printing services, the gross income for a given year could well exceed $125,000. After expenses though, particularly associated with hiring people to do the editing, proofreading, and other tasks, chances are this person would

be making around $80,000. To put this another way, I have only heard one credible claim of a person making over $100,000 per year, and that translator made clear the fact that he did nothing but translate for 365 days straight, in technical areas of defense technology from English to Russian. So yes, in principle, such income is possible, but in practice, you shouldn't expect it.

Q: What can I do if I want to earn more?
A: Translate more words or charge more per word if you are a freelancer, and develop relevant business skills if you are an in-house translator.

Q: I have so much work that I am thinking of starting a translation agency. Any advice?
A: Congratulations. I am thrilled to receive such a question. The only suggestion I can offer you is that I am available to do translation work... but seriously, I suggest you consult with any and all community services for people starting a business, as well as checking with an attorney to make sure you comply with all applicable laws, and so forth. In other words, move steadily and carefully through the process of going from a sole-proprietorship to a corporate entity with employees and contractors.

Preparation for the Field

Q: How do I know when my language skills are good enough to translate?
A: The short answer is: your skills are good enough to translate when you can actually translate. In other words, try to translate something, for instance a copy of a financial report, a software guide, a research article in a scientific publication, or a legal brief. If you can work through the material at a rate of a couple thousand words of translated text within one day and without making any significant errors, you are probably ready to translate. Of course you may need to have a professional check your work to make certain that your success is real.

Q: What can I read to be better informed about the translation industry?

A: The Language Realm (www.languagerealm.com) is one place to start. In addition, there are a few publications that I strongly recommend you refer to regularly. They are *Multilingual Computing* and Accurapid's *Translation Journal*, both available online. In addition, the *ATA Chronicle* as well as publications from regional and chapter organizations like the NCTA are worthwhile from time to time. Also, Inttranews provides an excellent news portal for translators. Beyond these, you should be reading magazines, journals, and books related to the subjects you translate in, as well as keeping abreast of your languages through whatever means are available to you.

Q: Are there any textbooks on translation?
A: The question really is: Are there any textbooks on translation for your language combination and subject areas? The answer thus depends on which languages you know and what subjects you want to translate in. The short answer is no, if only because there are so few textbooks available, and most are of limited value, that you should assume none exist unless you hear otherwise. Posting a message on a discussion group devoted to translation in your language pair or subject area should get you an answer particular to your needs. You can also search Amazon and other online booksellers, though I've found that the books that are offered have not been reviewed, so it's buyer beware.

Q: How important is being an expert in a subject area?
A: Very. You have to be able to translate material that is about something, and what most companies and agencies have a lot of these days is technical material in one form or another. Not only computer science, networks, and telecommunications, but also medical and biotechnology material, financial, and legal material are all common. Select something you like or have an aptitude for or background in and read, read, read.

Q: What about books to learn more about my subject areas?
A: Textbooks are appropriate. Buy recent editions of college- and even graduate-level textbooks for the subjects you plan on translating. If you plan to do financial translation, get books on accounting, managerial finance, tax law, and so forth. Then study the books as though you had to prepare to understand questions and even answer some, if not all, of them, and evaluate the language in the books with an eye toward translation. In other words, find and

169

learn words you do not already know, terminology you are unacquainted with, and particular phrases or idioms unique to that subject area. It will be easier to do this study in your native language of course, though there is considerable value to working through such books in all of your languages.

Q: What about software to study or practice my languages?
A: There are any number of good software packages for studying and learning languages, though most of them will not take you much beyond the level of an advanced college student. A translator needs to be far, far beyond that level, so the software might be a good way to review basics, keep up aural comprehension skills, and maybe study terminology (if the package in question includes a vocabulary module that you can add words to). It will not provide much in the way of practice for professional translation.

Q: How do I find good dictionaries?
A: I wish I knew. Most translators, particularly those working in technical fields, struggle with this problem. Years can pass before new terms in computers, finance, or what have you appear in print, so translators often rely on parallel reading to find good translations for new terms (parallel reading is the processing of reading two versions of one text), sharing their own term lists via the Web, and checking with clients and experts in the subject fields they work in. Good dictionaries do come along though, and they cause enough of a stir among translators that posting a message on a discussion group dedicated to translation, particularly one for your language pair or subject specialty, should yield useful information.

Business Practice

Q: I'm a freelance translator and my clients keep making unreasonable demands. How can I stop them?
A: Tell them to stop. Explain in simple, succinct terms what your limits are, then ask them to respect those limits, if only because you will provide them with higher quality work as a result. If they refuse to honor those requests, consider finding new clients.

Q: I am going to be late with a translation—

A: Stop right there. You should never submit any translation late. If you know you can't finish an assignment on time, tell you client or manager as soon as possible, preferably when you first receive the document. Service your client either by suggesting a new delivery schedule, perhaps with incremental deliveries, or by finding another translator to team up with to finish the assignment on time. Clients that receive work on time are happy clients, and happy clients give you more work.

Q: I don't like deadlines...
A: Then don't be a translator.

Q: My clients keep abandoning me. How can I keep them?
A: Do quality work at a fair price, submitting completed translations on time, and your clients will come back. Anything less and you run the risk of losing clients. Also, be sure that your clients really are abandoning you. Translation is a feast or famine industry; just because you don't hear from a client for a while doesn't mean you've been abandoned. They may just not have any work for you that week or month. Be patient, and have lots of clients.

Q: How many clients should I have as a freelance translator?
A: As many as afford you a good living, is the short answer. I suggest you follow the 80-20 rule, that is 80% of your work should come from 20% of your clients. This means you should have a few principle clients, three or four translation agencies, companies, or direct clients who keep you busy with a regular supply of work, and then another ten to twenty clients who come to you from time to time with smaller jobs. Also, keep track of your clients; no business relationship lasts forever, and you never know when one of your major clients may suddenly have little need for you. Always be on the lookout for a new major client, in other words, and for signs that a current major client is providing less work.

Q: How can I get rid of a bad client?
A: There are two approaches. One: Charge the client enough that whatever makes them "bad" becomes worth your time and effort. If they persist in using you, at least you'll feel better about working with them. Two: Tell the client you are too busy to accept work. Once you do this a few times, most clients will stop calling. Between these two strategies, you'll manage to get rid of all

undesirable clients. This problem, by the way, doesn't seem to happen very often.

Q: How long should I wait for payment?
A: When you accept a job, you should confirm with the client how long their pay cycle is. Add a few days to whatever you are told to allow for weekends, holidays, slow mail, and check-writer's cramp, and if payment doesn't arrive by that time, then politely inquire about your payment.

Q: What if I do everything you suggested in the book and still have not been paid?
A: If you have truly done everything, then you have been to court with a lawsuit for breech of contract and somehow managed to lose. Under those conditions, there is nothing I can suggest. If however you have merely been patient and sent some reminder letters or faxes, then you have to increase the pressure by threatening to take legal action, to involve the Better Business Bureau and local or national translation organizations, and to broadcast to all other translators the specifics of the client's behavior. This threat, which I've used only once in seven years, almost invariably results in prompt, courteous payment. If the threat does not result in payment, then follow through with the threat. You may still not get paid, that is for the courts to decide, but you will make a clear statement to the translation vendor.

Q: My client is deducting 10% from my invoiced amount, claiming I did a bad job. What do I do?
A: Did you do a good job? Did you request specifics about their claims? Did they back up the claim with an independent review? If you really did a bad job, accept the deduction gracefully, offer to make any changes or improvements for free, and hope you didn't just lose a client. If however you feel the client is being unreasonable in their assessment of your work, or worse even, perhaps trying to squeeze you to increase their profit margin, then you must prepare to fight. Demand firmly but politely to see detailed documentation of their claim, preferably reviewed by a third party. If they do not respond immediately, treat the situation like any other invoice in default. Issue the threats and see what happens. By the way, for newcomers to the profession, this happens very, very rarely. For reasons explained in the section on ethics,

translation agencies and vendors cannot afford to play these kinds of games.

Q: My client went out of business and I lost $16,000 in invoices. Can I do anything about it?
A: You what!?!? How could you possibly do that?! Never, never leave that much money outstanding. Invoice incrementally for all large projects, demand prompt payment, hold the rest of the project hostage if payment is not forthcoming, and if the client seems to be floundering, bail. Rats abandon sinking ships; no reason to stay around yourself. Okay, all that said, if the client really has gone into Chapter 11, then you have to join the line of creditors, usually a long one, and hope that as the company restructures or is sold off, some money comes your way. In other words, you should simply never get yourself into a situation like this in the first place.

Q: How can I find a good in-house position?
A: By looking far and wide in every available resource online and in print. Check Monster.com, Yahoo!'s job listings, translation directories and publications, and the websites of every translation company and agency to see if there are any openings suitable for you. Also, tell your acquaintances and associates that you are looking; since their circle of activity does not overlap with yours, they are more likely to hear of something than your friends are.

Taxes and Finances

Q: As a freelancer, do I have to pay taxes?
A: Yes. Translators, like all self-employed people, are required to file annual tax returns to the IRS, plus to any state or local agency where they live, if necessary. In addition, the IRS and state tax agencies expect a quarterly tax payment which represents an estimate of what you owe for that quarter. Called Estimated Tax Payments, these payments are due by April 15 for the quarter starting January 1 and ending March 31; by June 15 for the quarter starting April 1 and ending May 31; September 15 for the quarter starting June 1 and ending August 31; and January 15 for the quarter starting September 1 and ending December 31. There is a penalty for underpayment (including no payment) of estimated taxes, though if your estimates are close the penalty is minimal.

Q: Should I use an accountant or professional tax preparer?

A: You should do your taxes on your own at least once in your professional life, preferably using tax preparation software. This will help you understand the taxation process so that you can either plan and prepare your taxes more accurately on your own or work more efficiently with a professional in the future. Eventually your taxes may become sufficiently complicated that a professional is justified. To date I have not used one, though I know plenty of translators who do.

Q: Does the tax software really work?

A: Yes, it does. I have been using tax preparation software since 1993 and spend only about two hours per year doing my taxes. You of course have to keep accurate, efficient records throughout the year in order to have the tax preparation process go that smoothly, but you should have such records anyway, as a part of your business.

Q: How can I figure out what I owe?

A: Until you have all the numbers for the entire tax year, you can't figure out your tax burden precisely. You can however use the Tax Estimator on the Quicken web site (www.quicken.com) to get a rough estimate of your federal tax burden.

Q: What if a client doesn't send a 1099-MISC form? Say, for instance, they go out of business...

A: Employers that work with independent contractors are required by law to send out a 1099-MISC form by the end of February of the year after the tax year for all amounts in excess of $650.00. Note that the exact time and amount for a 1099-MISC form varies from year to year; consult with IRS forms and reference material for details. In any event, if you don't have a 1099-MISC form from an employer that owes you one, first contact the employer and see if that can get you one. If you can't find the employer, for instance, if the employer has gone out of business, contact the IRS. You will be given a 1099-MISC form to create for yourself, and you will have to supply evidence to justify the amount you place on it. Evidence includes check stubs and invoicing records. That will suffice for the IRS, which after you submit this mock 1099-MISC form will provide you with a confirmation letter some weeks later.

Q: Do I pay U.S. taxes on money I earn from translation vendors and clients in other countries?
A: Yes, unless there is a tax treaty to the contrary. Consult with a tax advisor or the IRS for details on how to report such income and if there are any special considerations.

Q: Are translators ever audited?
A: Yes they are. I know some who have been audited regularly and others who have been translating as freelancers for over 10 years without a single audit. Prepare your return neatly, accurately, and honestly, and your odds of an audit plummet. Also, an audit is not tantamount to the end of the world. If you have been honest and have all your paperwork, the process is a minor annoyance. If not, then you are in trouble and I can't help you.

Legal Issues

Q: Are translators ever sued?
A: I have heard about translators being threatened to be sued, but I personally know of no instance of a company actually suing a translator. Readers who know otherwise might do me the favor of filling me in on the details. Note that I first asked readers to share any such stories with my in the spring of 2000 and have yet to hear one as of fall, 2006. Based on what I have heard from attorneys, employment experts, and translation agencies, suing a translator just isn't worth the time and money.

Q: Should translators have professional liability insurance?
A: This doesn't seem useful at this point. The insurance itself is unlikely to cover you when you need it, and the fact you have coverage could make you more attractive target for a lawsuit. An effective policy to have with clients is that you will provide "good-faith, best effort" translations. Then as long as you do so, you shouldn't need liability insurance.

Q: Should I incorporate?
A: Perhaps. It depends on how you want to function as a business entity. For most freelance translators, incorporating is probably not worth the time and money required. For some though, it may well be. Consult with an attorney, or read through some books on small-

business management to get more ideas as to whether or not you should incorporate. I suspect you'll never have to, and I strongly urge you to work in the translation industry for a year or two before you do it, but ultimately it may be justified.

Technology and Equipment

Q: What software should I own?
A: A current version of Microsoft Office, including Word, PowerPoint, and Excel, is absolutely required. You should also have the usual collection of browsers and email clients, compression software, and any text utilities or fonts necessary for your languages. If you are self-employed, you will need business software to produce invoices and track your accounts, terminology management software either in the form of a general database application like Microsoft Access or Filemaker Pro or in a dedicated system, and MAT software like Trados or Catalyst, depending on your languages, is useful if not vital.

Q: What about machine translation? Why don't I just pump the source document into MT software and send the client the result?
A: Give it a try. See if the client contacts you again. Seriously though, the software just isn't good enough for much beyond basic texts whose quality isn't important. Try the free versions available online to give yourself an idea of what the output is like.

Q: What about dictating translations? My wrists and hands hurt...
A: My wrists and hands hurt, too, from time to time. And I do use dictation software, specifically Dragon Systems' Naturally Speaking (most of my work, and a lot of this book, was dictated, by the way). I find the software very efficient and accurate, and easy to use. Prior versions had difficulty with foreign names, obscure terms, and formatting. Though these issues remain, the software has a much better vocabulary now, and strong formatting tools. Also, it is compatible with most major word processors, particular Microsoft Word. So if you want to rest your arms or have developed a repetitive strain injury, this is a viable option.

Q: My child stuffed a peanut butter sandwich into my CD drive, and now I can't finish my translation...

A: Children and business computers do not mix. I have seen 12-year-olds take down fault-tolerant Cray Supercomputers, and I myself as a small child managed to crash more than one mini-computer. If at all possible, keep your business system away from younger family members and household pets. If not possible, purchase and use a utility that lets you lock out people and effectively shut down the computer when you are not using it. And, of course, keep backups of all your work so that you lose the absolute minimum possible should anything go wrong.

Q: Should I get MAT software like Trados or Catalyst?
A: That depends on what languages you work with and what kind of material you are translating. In general, if you are working on documents that represent new versions of older material in Romance or Germanic languages, then MAT will probably be essential; your clients may even insist you have one or more MAT packages. By contrast, if you are translating original research from Japanese to English, MAT software will not be at all useful. For more ideas on this subject, see the section on MAT software in Home Office.

Accreditation and Professional Organizations

Q: Is the ATA exam worth taking?
A: Perhaps. Many translation vendors view the ATA exam with some skepticism, in part because the exam is so brief and general as to provide only a minimal assessment of a translator's skills, and in part because the grading of the exam is highly subjective, and therefore some skilled, experienced translators do not pass, while less capable individuals pass. Also, the exam is expensive, requiring you to become an ATA member, then pay a fee to take the first tier or the exam, then another fee to take the second tier, and finally to keep your membership active if you want to claim accreditation. On the other hand, the ATA exam is a recognized credential, one of the few available in the United States, and so for a new translator who has no academic training, certification, or any other evidence of translation ability, it is probably worthwhile.

Q: Are there other exams?
A: Yes. The U.S. State Department has exams for interpreters, which could be used to demonstrate translation ability because of

the mistaken idea that those who can interpret can translate. The United Nations also offers exams, though the requirements for taking those exams preclude all but the most experienced translators from applying. There are schools in the country that offer various forms of academic training, with a degree or certification at the end of the process, and so are worth considering for some people.

Q: Is the ATA worth joining?
A: For newcomers to the profession, yes. Although some argue that the ATA does not offer much for its membership fees and many translators seem to feel that participating in the local chapter organizations gives them far more of what they need and choose not to join the ATA, there are plenty of translators who enjoy and seem to benefit from their ATA membership. If you plan to take the ATA certification exam, you will have to join.

Q: Can a translator succeed without joining any organizations?
A: Yes, absolutely. The ATA and various chapter organizations offer many services of varying degrees of utility, but none of it is indispensable.

Miscellaneous Issues

Q: Should I learn another language? Any in particular?
A: You already know how much time and effort learning a language is, so I suggest you pick one that inspires you. But also pick one that has some reasonable chance of being in demand. The obvious strong languages in the next five to ten years include Arabic, Chinese, Hindi, Japanese, Korean, Portuguese, and Russian, among others.

Q: I am just starting to think about being a translator? Any advice?
A: Start learning a foreign language, preferably Arabic, Chinese, Farsi, Japanese, Korean, or Russian. These languages are mostly likely in the next ten to twenty years to provide good job opportunities and steady income. Next, pick a subject you like and get to know it well, because translators specialize, and you need to become an expert in one or several related subjects. Finally, develop strong technical skills, including computer programming if possible. This will serve you well as the technology translators use evolves.

Q: I want to improve my skills. What can I do?

A: Take classes in the subjects you want to improve in. Most community colleges and many universities offer a wide range of classes to the public through extension or continuing education programs. Some classes can be had online now, too. There is no reason not to continue your education, especially with the advent of the Web.

Q: What about weekend workshops?

A: These can be useful, but be careful. There are translators and others in the industry who offer workshops in lieu of actually translating, which makes me wonder why they aren't translating. If the workshop is a part of a larger program, an offering by the ATA or at least certified for ATA continuing education credits, then it should be worth your time and money. If you can find others who have taken the workshop, then you'll get the best information possible.

Q: How can I contact you with a question?

A: Email me at rbchriss@languagerealm.com, or use the contact form on the Language Realm website (www.languagerealm.com). I will respond as quickly as I can.

Resources

This section of the book is meant to help you figure out where to go next for more information. All information is accurate as of this writing. A great deal of useful information can be found from the websites, journals (online and print), news portals, and books listed below. I hope you'll explore at least a few of them. As the industry changes are your career evolves, you will need good sources of information, and these are among my favorites. Of course I included the companion website for this book in this section, and you can contact me there or via rbchriss@languagerealm.com if you have any questions about this section, or suggestions for new additions.

ATA and Chapter Associations

American Translators Association
225 Reinekers Lane, Suite 590
Alexandria, VA 22314
(703) 683-6100
ata@atanet.org
www.atanet.org

Atlanta Association of Interpreters and Translators (AAIT)
P.O. Box 12172
Atlanta, GA 30355
(404) 729-4036
AAITInfo@aait.org
www.aait.org

Carolina Association of Translators and Interpreters (CATI)
232 Branch Hill Drive
Elgin, SC 29045
(201) 953-4621
catiadmin@catiweb.org

Resources

www.catiweb.org

Delaware Valley Translators Association (DVTA)
606 John Anthony Drive
West Chester, PA 19382
contactDVTA@cs.com
www.dvta.org

Florida Chapter of ATA (FLATA)
7891 W Flagler Street, #347
Miami, FL 33144
(305) 274-3434
President@atafl.org
www.atafl.org

Michigan Translators/Interpreters Network (MiTiN)
P.O. Box 852
Novi, MI 48376-0852
(586) 778-7304
info@mitinweb.org
www.mitinweb.org

Mid-America Chapter of ATA (MICATA)
6600 NW Sweetbriar Lane
Kansas City, MO 64151
(816) 741-9441
translate@kc.rr.com
www.ata-micata.org

Midwest Association of Translators and Interpreters (MATI)
IUPUI
Dept of World Languages & Cultures
425 University Boulevard
Indianapolis, IN 46202
(317) 273-8957
eardema@iupui.edu
www.matiata.org

National Capital Area Chapter of ATA (NCATA)
P.O. Box 5757
Washington, DC 20016-5757

(703) 255-9290
alexandrarb@yahoo.com
www.ncata.org

New York Circle of Translators (NYCT)
P.O. Box 4051
Grand Central Station
New York, NY 10163-4051
(212) 334-3060
president@nyctranslators.org
www.nyctranslators.org

Northeast Ohio Translators Association (NOTA)
33425 Bainbridge Road
Solon, OH 44139
(440) 519-0161
pres@ohiotranslators.org
www.ohiotranslators.org

Northern California Translators Association (NCTA)
P.O. Box 14015
Berkeley, CA 94712-5015
(510) 845-8712
ncta@ncta.org
www.ncta.org

Northwest Translators and Interpreters Society (NOTIS)
P.O. Box 25301
Seattle, WA 98165-2201
(206) 382-5642
info@notisnet.org
www.notisnet.org

Upper Midwest Translators and Interpreters Association (UMTIA)
Minnesota Translation Lab
University of Minnesota
218 Nolte Center
Minneapolis, MN 55455
(612) 625-3096
mtl@tc.umn.edu
www.umtia.com

ATA Affiliates

Austin Area Translators and Interpreters Association (AATIA)
P.O. Box 13331
Austin, TX 78711-3331
(512) 707-3900
president@aatia.org
www.aatia.org

Houston Interpreters and Translators Association (HITA)
P.O. Box 421343
Houston, TX 77242-1343
(713) 202-6169
www.hitagroup.org

Iowa Interpreters and Translators Association (IITA)
P.O. Box 7631
Urbandale, IA 50323
(515) 865-3873
info@iitanet.org
www.iitanet.org

Utah Translators and Interpreters Association (UTIA)
625 N 600 W
American Fork, UT 84003
(801) 492-1226
katyab@xmission.com

Professional Associations for Translators

The American Association of Language Specialists (TAALS)
admin@taals.net
www.taals.net

American Literary Translators Association (ALTA)
P.O. Box 830688
Richardson, TX 75083-0688
(972) 883-2093
jdickey@utdallas.edu

American Medical Writers Association
40 W Gude Drive, Suite 101
Rockville, MD 20850
(301) 294-5303
amwa@amwa.org
www.amwa.org

AIIC (International Association of Conference Interpreters)
10, avenue de Sécheron
CH - 1202 Geneva, Switzerland
+41 22 908 15 40
info@aiic.net
www.aiic.net

The California Court Interpreters Association (CCIA)
345 S. Highway 101, Suite D
Encinitas, CA 92024
(760) 635-0273
ccia345@earthlink.net
www.ccia.org

Canadian Translators and Interpreters Council
1, rue Nicholas Street
bureau 1202
Ottawa, Canada K1N 7B7
(613) 562-0379
ctic@on.aibn.com

Chicago Area Translators and Interpreters Association (CHICATA)
P.O. Box 804595
Chicago, IL 60680-4107
(312) 836-0961
webmaster@chicata.org

Colorado Translators Association (CTA)
941 Cedwick Street
Lafayette, CO 80026
(720) 890-7934
kathy@kdtranslations.com
www.cta-web.org

Delaware Translators' Network (DTN)

Resources

2401 Pennsylvania Avenue, #912
Wilmington, DE 19806
(302) 655-5368
levinx@cs.com

El Paso Interpreters and Translators Association (EPITA)
P.O. Box 27157
El Paso, TX 79926
(915) 598-4757
mhogan@elp.rr.com

Fédération Internationale des Traducteurs/International Federation
of Translators (FIT)
2021, Union Avenue, Suite 1108
Montréal, Québec, H3A 2S9
Canada
(514) 845-0413
secretariat@fit-ift.org
www.fit-ift.org

GALA: Globalization and Localization Association
23 Main Street
Andover, Massachusetts 01810
(206) 329-2596
www.gala-global.org

Japan Association of Translators
2-19-15-808, Shibuya, Shibuya-ku
Tokyo 150-0002, Japan
www.jat.org

Literary Translators' Association of Canada
SB 335 Concordia University
1455, boul. de Maisonneuve ouest
Montreal (Quebec)
H3G 1M8
(514) 848-8702
info@attlc-ltac.org
www.attlc-ltac.org

Localization Industry Standards Association (LISA)
7, rte du Monastere

1173 Fechy - Switzerland
+41 21 821 32 10
lisa@lisa.org
www.lisa.org

Metroplex Interpreters and Translators Association (MITA)
712 Cornfield Drive
Arlington, TX 76017
(817) 417-4747
www.dfw-mita.com

National Association of Judiciary Interpreters and Translators
(NAJIT)
603 Stewart Street, Suite 610
Seattle, WA 98101
(206) 267-2300
headquarters@najit.org
www.najit.org

New England Translators Association (NETA)
672 Salls Road
Greensborough Bend, VT 05842
(802) 533-9228
info@netaweb.org
www.netaweb.org

New Mexico Translators and Interpreters Association (NMTIA)
P.O. Box 36263
Albuquerque, NM 87176
(505) 352-9258
uweschroeter@comcast.net
www.cybermesa.com/~nmtia

Society for Technical Communication (STC)
901 N Stuart Street, Suite 904
Arlington, VA 22203-1822
(703) 522-4114
www.stc.org

Society of Translators and Interpreters of British Columbia (STIBC)
850 West Hastings Street
Suite 514, Box 34

Vancouver, BC, V6C 1E1
Canada
(604) 684-2940
office@stibc.org
www.stibc.org

The Translators and Interpreters Guild (TTIG)
962 Wayne Avenue, #500
Silver Spring, MD 20910-4432
(301) 563-6450 or (866) 563-6456
info@ttig.org
www.ttig.org/

Washington State Court Interpreters and Translators Society (WITS)
P.O. Box 1012
Seattle, WA 98111-1012
(206) 382-5690
www.witsnet.org

Job Sources

General Job Sources:

Monster.com (and its partner sites for countries around the world)
Jobdango.com
Yahoo.com (which has a large, searchable jobs area)
Hotjobs.com

Freelance/In-House Job Sources:

www.proz.com
www.translatorscafe.com
www.aquarius.net
www.bilingualsearch.com
www.botranslators.com
www.translationdirectory.com
www.globtra.com
www.transref.org
www.elance.com

Government Jobs (Including Military and Intelligence Work)

www.defendingamerica.org
www.nvtc.gov (National Virtual Translation Center)
www.goarmy.com (U.S. Army)
www.navyjobs.com (U.S. Navy)
www.airforce.com (U.S. Air Force)
www.usmc.com (U.S. Marine Corps.)
www.coastguard.com (Coast Guard)
www.cia.gov (CIA: Central Intelligence Agency)
www.nsa.gov (NSA: National Security Agency)
www.fbi.gov (FBI: Federal Bureau of Investigation)
www.usajobs.gov (Civil Service jobs)
www.usajobs.opm.gov (Civil Service jobs with the military)

The above represents just the tip of the iceberg for possible translation jobs, freelance or in-house. Much more can be found through simple web searches using keywords like "translation agency" or "translation company", by checking the job offerings on the websites of the ATA and other professional associations, by looking at the job listings in your local newspaper (online edition), and by reading the advertisements on translation websites, most of which are from translation agencies or companies.

Schools for Translation Training

Degree Programs

Monterey Institute of International Studies (MIIS) (www.miis.edu) offers a M.A. in Translation, in Translation and Interpretation, and in Conference Interpretation. Located in California (US), the program includes Spanish, French, German, Russian, Korean, Chinese, and Japanese.

Kent State University (http://appling.kent.edu/IAL-Programs.htm) offers an M.A. specializing in translation. Located in Ohio, the program offers French, German, Japanese, Russian, or Spanish, and also offers a doctorate (Ph.D.) in translation studies for Spanish, French, and German.

Resources

Graduate School, College of Charleston
(http://www.cofc.edu/~legalint/) offers a M.A. in Bilingual Legal Interpreting. The program is undergoing a revision, so interested people should check the Web site and email the director.

University of Washington, Seattle (http://tjp.washington.edu/main/), offers a Technical Masters of Japanese. Located in Seattle, Washington (US), the program focuses on the translation of Japanese and English technical material and assumes a strong scientific or engineering background.

University of Wisconsin Madison
(http://metj.engr.wisc.edu/index.lasso) offers a Master's of Engineering in Technical Japanese, a Certificate of Technical Japanese Studies, and other advanced language training.

Binghamton University (SUNY) (http://trip.binghamton.edu/) offers TRIP, the Translation Research & Instruction Program, the only academic program in the U.S. to offer a doctorate in translation and related studies. Note that this program is for scholars, not individuals looking to develop skills as professional translators or interpreters.

Certificate Programs

Bellevue Community College
(http://www.conted.bcc.ctc.edu/translation/ticert.asp) offers has a Translation and Interpretation Certificate program. Located near Seattle, Washington (US), the program focuses on basic training and includes some language-specific coursework.

New York University
(http://www.scps.nyu.edu/departments/department.jsp?deptId=11)
offers certificate programs in translation, court interpreting, and medical interpreting, as well as certificate programs in a variety of major languages

University of California at San Diego (UCSD) Extension (http://www.extension.ucsd.edu/programs/index.cfm?vAction=cert Detail&vCertificateID=83&vStudyAreaID=11) offers a Certificate Program for Spanish/English translation and interpretation.

University of Wisconsin Milwaukee
(http://www.uwm.edu/Dept/GCIT/index.html) offers a Graduate
Certificate in Translation for French, German, and Spanish.

University of Florida
(http://www.translationstudies.ufl.edu/program.shtml) offers a
Translation Studies Certificate Program for people with a Bachelor's
degree, or those who will soon complete one, in a wide variety of
languages.

Miami Dade College
(http://www.mdc.edu/iac/AcademicPrograms/ESL_Foreign_lang/tra
nslation_prog.asp) offers, though its InterAmerican Campus, an
Associates Degree and two certificate programs in translation and
interpretation for English/Spanish and English/Haitian Creole.

Informational Websites

The Language Realm (the companion website for this book)
www.languagerealm.com

Occupational Outlook Handbook (U.S. Department of Labor,
Bureau of Statistics)
www.bls.gov/oco/ocos175.htm

Interagency Language Roundtable
www.govtilr.org/ILRscale1.htm

Translation Journal from Accurapid
A very interesting quarterly publication with articles about
translation and interpretation
www.accurapid.com/journal

Multilingual Computing
An online and print journal covering technology in the translation
industry and localization business.
www.multilingual.com

Inttranews

Resources

A web portal for news about translation, interpretation, language, linguistics, and related subjects
http://inttranews.inttra.net/cgi-bin/index.cgi

Recommended Reading

A Practical Guide to Software Localization, by Bert Essenlink

Handbook of Terminology Management: Basic Aspects of Terminology Management, by Sue Ellen Wright, and Gerhard Budin

If This Be Treason: Translation and Its Discontents, A Memoir, by Gregory Rabassa

In Other Words: A Coursebook on Translation, by Mona Bakr

On Writing Well, by William Zinser

The Art of Translation, by Theodore Savory

The Elements of Style, by William Strunk and E.B. White

Glossary of Terms

The glossary here includes not only various terms used in the book, but also ones that you are likely to encounter as you start working as a translator, read journals or other publications, talk with other professionals, and deal with various technologies. A more extensive glossary that includes linguistic and language terminology is available on the Language Realm (www.languagerealm.com).

A language The language a person is most proficient in, typically the person's native language. Although some people can have two A languages as a result of birth and upbringing, this is exceedingly rare.

Accredited translator A translator who has received certification or accreditation from a professional association. The ATA now refers to certified translators, meaning those that have passed the ATA exam. But with the ATA certification is not a requirement for membership, though with other organizations it is. Some organizations offer certification based on experience or education, though the ATA does not.

Ad hoc interpreting A form of interpretation for informal conversations that is used in business meetings, during phone calls or site visits, and at social events. Consecutive interpreting may be used, but whispering interpreting is more common.

Adaptation The rewriting of a source text in the target language so that the result does not appear to be a translation. This is frequently done with user's guides, marketing and promotional materials, and other content that cannot succeed as a strait translation.

AIIC Acronym for the Association Internationale des Interprets de Conference (the official name is in French). Pronounced "ay-eek" by most people in English, this is the premier organization for conference interpreters in the world. Membership comes to those who have worked long and hard at a high level as interpreters.

Alignment The creation of equivalent segments (meaning units) between a source text and the corresponding target text. The resulting table or database of equivalents can then be used as a translation memory with tools such as Trados or Wordfast. Alignment allows for previous translations to be used without such software, however. But even with MAT software, hands-on work is still required to complete the translation.

Ambiguity The bane of translators, and a frequent problem in source texts. Most source texts are not well written, and have ambiguous phrases. The translator is stuck having to guess, or when possible, contact the writer of the source text for clarification.

ATA Acronym for the American Translators' Association, a national organization of and for translators and interpreters in the United States. It provides services such as a monthly publication, an annual conference, special interest groups, and an online directory of its members.

Automatic recognition An electronic dictionary, usually associated with MAT tools, finds an equivalent in the target language for a term in the source language, assuming such a pair exists in the dictionary. In technical translation, this process ensures terminological consistency throughout the entire text, which is especially useful when several translators are working on the text.

Automatic translation Another phrase for machine translation, though the translation is only automatic after thousands of hours of labor have produced multi-language dictionaries, linguistic rules for analysis of the source text, or gigantic corpuses of parallel texts in the source and target language, all leveraged by the vast processing power of modern computers. The results are still disappointing and cannot replace the work of well-trained, experienced human translators.

B language A language a person has close to native proficiency in. Here, proficiency includes reading, writing, listening, and speaking skills.

Back translation A process in which a translator takes a text (original or translated) which is written in a language with which the reader is assumed to be unfamiliar and translating it as literally as possible into English. How literally the text is translated depends on the final purpose of the translated text.

C language A language a person has a high level of proficiency in, but not near native proficiency. Here, proficiency includes reading, writing, listening, and speaking skills.

Callout A label with an arrow or line pointing to something, usually a graphic or figure embedded in the source text and that the translator cannot access through software. This frequently is used in the translation of patents and other technical documentation; the production staff will use the callouts to assemble a target-language version of the graphic or figure.

CAT Acronym for Computer-Aided Translation, an approach to translation in which computer technology automates or supports translators in the process of translation between or among natural languages.

CJKV Abbreviation for Chinese, Japanese, Korean, and Vietnamese. A standard abbreviation used in the translation and localization industries to refer to these four languages.

Conference interpreter An interpreter who works at conferences, usually large, international events, providing simultaneous and sometimes consecutive interpretation in two or more languages. In Europe, most conference interpreters have three languages, and many have four. In Asia, the norm is two, though more and more interpreters offer three.

Consecutive interpreting Consecutive interpreting is a mode of interpreting in which the interpreter listens to the speaker while taking notes, then reproduces the speaker's speech in the target language. Consecutive interpreting is considered the most accurate form of interpretation, but also the most time-intensive, because the total time for an interpreted speech is at least double speaker time. Often abbreviated "consec" when people are talking about it.

Controlled language A form of language in which vocabulary is restricted and structures and grammar are controlled. Controlled language is often used in technical materials to make them more accessible, or is used to prepare a text for machine translation.

Copywriting The production of advertising or publicity copy. Advertising copy does not translate well because of cultural and social factors that vary substantially from one nation to another. Local agencies should always produce copy for their own markets.

Court interpreter An interpreter with an excellent knowledge of the law and legal proceedings who provides interpretation in legal contexts, including depositions, courtroom proceedings, and prison interviews. Requirements for certification vary from region to region, and passing a court interpreter exam is a mark of achievement, and often a path to a stable workflow.

Critical Need Foreign Languages Defined in the National Security Language Initiative as languages such as Arabic, Chinese, Russian, Hindi, Farsi, that are recognized by the U.S. government as being very important in present and future international relations and security issues.

DBCS Abbreviation for Double Byte Character Set. A system for encoding characters that uses one or two bytes. Japanese, Chinese, and Korean, among others, use a double byte system, whereas the Roman alphabet can be encoded using just one byte, and so is called a single byte character set.

Desktop Publishing Often abbreviated DTP, this is the process of creating the layout of a document, particularly a newspaper, magazine, or journal. Desktop publishing is sometimes offered by translators and translation companies/agencies as a value-added service to provide a one-stop solution for customers' publishing needs. They will usually have the special equipment required to handle languages that use different writing systems.

FAHQT Abbreviation for Fully Automatic High Quality Translation. An acronym used to refer to the as-yet unachieved, and some argue impossible, machine translation system whose output is as good as or better than a human translator's.

FIGS Abbreviation for French, Italian, German, and Spanish. A standard abbreviation used in the translation and localization industries to refer to the above languages as a group.

Free translation A translation in which the translator focuses more on the overall meaning of the text than the exact wording. It is the opposite of a literal translation, and is most often used in marcom, that is, marketing and communications, where the idea is most important, and the structure or exact wording of the original can be ignored.

Freelance translator A self-employed translator who works for translation agencies, translation companies, or directly for their own clients. Freelance translators usually specialize in one or several related fields. Much of the translation industry in the United States is freelance, though in Europe this is less the case.

Fuzzy matching A technique for finding pairs of words or phrases that are close but not exact matches. This process is often used in electronic dictionaries or in MAT software. The translator can thus get a useful idea for a translation based on existing material, even if an exact translation does not exist in the translation memories, corpuses, or standard dictionaries. The exact value of the process varies from translation to translation, and from language to language.

GILT Abbreviation for Globalization, Internationalization, Localization, and Translation. A convenient acronym to describe everything going on in and around the translation industry and profession.

Gisting The process of creating a rough or outline version of a translation to give general information about the subject and content of the source material. Gisting is less expensive and faster than a full translation, and is often used to find out if a text is worth translating. Some machine translation systems are capable of usable gisting, depending on the source text and the needs of the translation consumer.

Globalization The process of preparing software, a web site, or other product or service so that modifications that occur during the localization process do not interfere with its function. This process includes data formats, screen space for dialog boxes, menus, or windows, and special functions to replace icons and other symbols as appropriate.

Glossary A specialized dictionary in one or more languages for a particular purpose. It is often little more than a word list, though sometimes includes definitions, examples of usage, and additional information about the entries.

Internationalization The process of preparing, at a technical or design level, a product, usually software or hardware, for localization. Internationalization is thus part of globalization, and usually does not involve translators directly. Sometimes written i18n because there are 18 letters between the 'i' and the 'n'.

Leverage This is a process performed by MAT systems in which elements from a previous translation are automatically incorporated into new versions of a document.

LGP Abbreviation for Language for General Purposes. The everyday language that comprises most chitchat, conversations with friends, or text in a novel. Translators rarely deal with LGP as compared to how often they work with Language for Special Purposes (c.f.: LSP below).

Liaison interpreter An interpreter who provides, usually in consecutive interpretation mode, interpretation between two languages in both directions. Such interpreters are often employed by or hired by the host organization and may also act as a facilitator in negotiations or perform public relations duties.

LISA Abbreviation for the Localization Industry Standards Association. Founded in 1990 as a non-profit association, LISA is an organization for the GILT (Globalization, Internationalization, Localization, and Translation) business communities. Over 400 leading IT manufacturers and solutions providers, along with industry professionals and an increasing number of vertical market corporations with an international business focus, have helped establish LISA best practice guidelines and language-technology standards for enterprise globalization.

Literal translation A translation that closely follows the wording and structure of the source text. A literal translation is usually recognizable as a translation (just consider the consumer electronics manuals from the 1980s and 90s), and is usually avoided unless there is a specific need for one.

Literary translator A translator who specializes in the translation of literature, such as fiction, biographies and poetry. Most literary translators are academics with doctorates in their languages and literature they work with, and many make a living teaching while earning some income from their translation work.

Language of lesser diffusion Abbreviated LLD, this is a convenient and politically polite way to refer to a language spoken by a relatively small population. Examples include Dutch, Greek, and Welsh.

Localization The process of adapting a product, typically software or a Web site, to make it consistent with what another market expects of such products. This process includes the translation of all documentation (manuals, online help, Web-based help, advertising), the adaptation of various screens and dialog boxes, keyboard shortcuts, icons and images, and even to some extent the nature of the content itself. Sometimes written l10n (because there are 10 letters between the 'l' and the 'n'), this is the origin of the name Lionbridge.

LSP Abbreviation for Language for Special Purposes. Refers to any part of a language that is used for a particular purpose, such as the language used in medicine, law, or localization. Such language is higher-level in its demand for terminology, style, and knowledge to use it accurately. Most translation involves LSP.

Machine Translation (MT) The use of computer software and sometimes dedicated hardware to translate human languages with, at least ideally, no human involvement. At present this ideal has not been achieved; pre- and post-editing of MT texts is still essential. MT at its best can provide translations useful for getting the gist of the material. At its worst, it produces "word salad."

MAT Abbreviation for Machine-Assisted Translation, which is the use of computer software to accelerate, streamline, or otherwise make the translation process more efficient and cost-effective. Common MAT products include Trados and Catalyst.

Medical interpreting A form of interpreting performed in hospitals, clinics, physicians' offices and other medical settings, in which the interpreter works between the doctor or nurse and the patient, and often the family. Medical interpreting has become controversial, with some states in the U.S. starting to regulate who can interpret.

MLV Abbreviation for Multi-Language Vendor. An MLV is a translation vendor that handles more than one language combination. Most translation vendors are now MLVs, with the exception, for instance, of specialized organizations that sit in a niche market.

MT Abbreviation for Machine Translation (see above).

OLIF Abbreviation for the Open Lexicon Interchange Format. This is a method for exchanging terminological and lexical data.

Parallel text A text in the source or target language that is similar to the text to be translated, especially for terminology and subject matter. This can include earlier translations of the same text or type of text.

Pivot language the language shared by a team of interpreters, or sometimes translators, and used in common. For instance, at many international conferences, a delegate who speaks a less common language such as Kannada or Yoruba will have an interpreter who works between the delegate's language and English. All the other interpreters will work between English and their target language, such as French, Russian, Arabic, or Chinese. Thus, English is the pivot language here, and in most instances at international conferences, English is used in this way.

Pre-translation The process of preparing a text for translation, usually machine translation. This can include spell-checking the source text, converting file formats for the MT system, preparing specialized dictionaries based on the source text, and other forms of analysis of the source text. Such effort is only justified when the translation project is large.

Proofreading This is the process of checking spelling, grammar and syntax, as well as the general coherency and integrity of the target text. Proofreading is essential to producing a quality translation; no translator produces error-free work all the time, and this process is the way to correct the inevitable problems that occur during translation.

Register A variety of language that a language user considers appropriate to a specific situation. The subject of the language, the tone of its delivery, and the techniques used to deliver the language represent three principle factors in register.

Repetition rate This is a percentage representing the amount of terms and segments that are repeated in a text. The repetition rate is important in MAT systems because it determines in advance how much of the text will only need to be translated once.

Segment A unit of language, usually a phrase, that results after MAT software divides the source text into chunks to create a translation memory. Rules based on punctuation and other syntactical considerations govern the process of segmentation.

Sight translation A mode of translation (or interpretation, depending on the situation) in which you produce orally in a target language what you read in a source text. Sight is useful not only for interpretation when a speaker will be reading from a prepared text (so-called sight/simul) but also for translators who are asked to tell someone what a particular chunk of text says. In addition, strong sight skills improve translation speed and accuracy, and are invaluable for interpreters. Abbreviated "sight" often.

Simultaneous interpretation Often called simul for short, this is a mode of interpretation in which the interpreter listens to the speaker over a closed-circuit audio system, reproducing the speaker's speech as the speaker speaks. Usually, a simul interpreter sits in a booth or other sound-proof environment, using headphones to listen and a microphone to speak. Simul is considered the fastest mode of interpreting, but accuracy is lower than that seen for consecutive interpreting.

SLV Abbreviation for Single-Language Vendor. An SLV is a translation vendor that handles only one language combination. SLVs tend to be smaller than MLVS, as one would expect. SLVs are becoming progressively rarer, though they do still exist in some niche markets.

SME Abbreviation for Subject Matter Expert. Someone who is considered an expert in their particular field, usually by virtue of a combination of academic or other form of formal training and practical, professional experience.

Source In translation, and as opposed to "target", the term "source" defines everything connected to the language of the text to be translated.

Source text analysis A process performed before translation to optimize the translation project. The process determines the length, scope, and problems the translation will present, and the optimum solutions. During this process, term lists, dictionaries, and translation memories may be compiled, a word count performed, repetition rate determined, and a provisional glossary created. Source text analysis is worthwhile particularly when the translation project is large, and when resources such as glossaries, translation memories, and MAT are involved.

Specialized language competence This represents familiarity with the relevant subject matter and command of its special language conventions, in particular writing style and terminology.

Standard line This is a standard measure of the size of a text as used in Europe. The United States tends to work on a per-word basis. The standard line varies from country to country and language to language. Translation projects are priced based on the word count in the United States and the line in Europe.

Target This term refers to everything related to the language which the text will be translated into. Its opposite is source. So the source text in the source language is translated into the target text in the target language. Typically, but not always, the target language is the translator's native language.

TDB Abbreviation for Translation Database. A software application, or part of a software application, that stores and codes terms in dictionaries. TermMarker, Termstar from STAR and Multiterm from Trados are examples. Some translators and translation companies build their own TDB using database software.

Technical translation The translation of scientific, medical, engineering, and related material. Content varies from user documentation, engineering specifications, and research papers, to patents, clinical trials, and ISO 9000 compliance materials. Technical translators tend to have an extensive knowledge of science and engineering, and often use MAT tools to maintain terminological consistency.

Text expansion An increase in the length of the target text as compared to the source text. This has little effect on translators, except as far as pricing, but must be given due consideration by graphic artists and desktop publishers who want to use the same format or templates for both the source text and translated text. Similarly, text expansion must be taken into consideration when translating software, since dialog boxes and windows may have to be resized to accommodate the translated text.

Text function This represents the purpose of the text: an instruction manual, sales material, engineering specifications. Translators base vocabulary and style choices on text function, so knowing this beforehand is quite useful.

TMX Abbreviation for Translation memory exchange format, a file format to make the exchange of translation memory data between different software packages easier and without any loss of data. Most major translation memory packages now support TMX.

Translation The process of rendering written text from one language into another while both retaining all the content of the original and producing a natural-sounding result in the result.

Translation agency A translation agency provides translation and interpreting services, acting as a middleman and sometimes broker between customers and freelance translators. Many offer value-added services such as typesetting, publishing, and project management. The term is often used interchangeably with translation company.

Translation company A translation company specializes in translation services using mainly in-house translators. Some specialize in a particular field, including legal, medical, or technical, and most offer value-added services such as typesetting, publishing, and project management. The term is often used interchangeably with translation agency.

Translation management Abbreviated TM, and not to be confused with translation memory, this is a blanket term to refer to the entire process of managing a translation project. Most often it refers to a large-scale project, such as localization of software, in which a large source document is being translated into several target languages.

Translation memory Abbreviated TM, a translation memory is a database which stores a source text and the corresponding target text in the form of translation units. Translation memory, the basis of MAT software, makes it possible to automatically find passages that have been translated previously, or to find modified passages for the translator to work on. Also a generic way of referring to IBM's Translation Manager software.

Translation unit A translation unit consists of the source segment and the corresponding target segment, recorded as equivalents in a database used by translation memories.

Translator A person who renders written text from one or more languages into a different language, usually his native language (or language of habitual use). Some translator offers other services, such as desktop publishing or proofreading, or even interpreting.

Whispering interpreting This is similar to simultaneous interpreting, but the interpreter works without technology, instead sitting next to or behind the listener and whispering the interpretation.

Word count This is a standard measure of the size of a text, usually based on the word-count feature available in all modern word processing software packages. Translation projects are often priced on a per-word basis in the United States.

Index

CPSIA information can be obtained at www.ICGtesting.com
Printed in the USA
LVOW081601130113

315521LV00002B/314/A